THE STILL SMALL VOICE

The Story of Jewish Ethics

BOOK ONE

William B. Silverman

BEHRMAN HOUSE, INC. *Publishers, New York*

To Pearl, Joel, and Eldon

ILLUSTRATIONS BY *Howard Simon*

FIFTH PRINTING, 1961

Copyright 1955 by William B. Silverman

Published by Behrman House, Inc.
1261 Broadway, New York 1

MANUFACTURED IN THE UNITED STATES OF AMERICA

Library of Congress Catalog Card Number: 55-11143

FOREWORD

The purpose of this volume is to offer an introduction to the subject of applied Jewish Ethics. Utilizing the technique of an imaginary classroom situation, students search for the answer to the mystery of the Still Small Voice. Each chapter provides a clue by offering moral insights derived from the Bible or Rabbinic Literature. The significance of Judaism as a way of life is highlighted by statements and quotations from contemporary Jewish thought and literature.

It is the hope of the author that this study of Jewish Ethics, motivated by provocative questions, pertinent case histories, and realistic problems confronting modern Jewish youth, may challenge the students to quest for the understanding of Judaism as a living faith that is applied to the synagogue, home, school, athletic field, human relations, and every aspect of life.

W. B. S.

ACKNOWLEDGMENTS

Grateful acknowledgment is here made to the following who have contributed to the preparation and publication of this volume:

Professor Sylvan Schwartzman and Rabbi Paul Steinberg, who read and evaluated the manuscript.

Mrs. Ben Loventhal, my secretary, who typed and prepared the manuscript for publication.

My students in religious school classes who provided the case histories, problems, and much of the motivation material by means of their frank discussion of the ethical questions of concern to modern Jewish youth.

The Bible and Rabbinic Literature for revealing the ethical precepts, moral values and sublime ideals of a God-seeking faith.

My devoted wife, Pearl, for her patience, encouragement, and love.

W. B. S.

CONTENTS

1. THE VOICE OF JACOB   1
The Mystery

2. THE VOICE OF GOD   17
Is God a Magician?

3. THE VOICE OF THE TORAH   35
Ethics of Jewish Law

4. THE VOICE AT SINAI   55
The Tablets That Never Grow Old

5. THE VOICE OF THE PROPHETS   72
Spokesmen of God

6. THE VOICE OF THE PSALMIST   98
The Holiness of Man

7. THE VOICE OF WISDOM   120
The Ethics of the Book of Proverbs

8. THE VOICE OF THE FATHERS   144
Ethics of the Pirke Aboth

9. THE VOICE OF THE RABBIS   165
The Ethics of the Talmud and Midrash

10. THE STILL, SMALL VOICE   196
Judaism in Action

1

THE VOICE OF JACOB

The Mystery

How It All Began

Have you ever cheated in an examination?

This may be an odd way to start a story, but it was because of cheating that an entire class tried to solve the mystery of the Still, Small Voice.

It happened in a religious school just like yours, to students who are very much like you and your friends. This is how it all began.

The class was writing furiously to complete the monthly quiz on history, when Rabbi Mayer saw a student glance hastily at a crumpled paper on the floor.

"Jonathan!" said the Rabbi. The class looked up, and buzzed. Jonathan was one of the class leaders, and some even said he was the Rabbi's favorite.

"Please give me the paper that interests you so much, Jonathan. Perhaps it will interest me too." The Rabbi's voice was quiet and calm.

The boy picked up the paper and walked slowly to the Rabbi's desk. Rabbi Mayer looked at the scrawled list of facts, names, and dates.

"Aren't these answers to the questions you thought I would ask, Jonathan?"

The bell rang, but no one moved.

Jonathan finally replied. "Yes, Rabbi. I'm sorry I cheated, but gosh—I'm not the only one. We've all been doing it for a long time. I just happened to get caught."

Rabbi Mayer turned to the class. "Is this true?"

The students looked down at their desks as if they had never seen them before. The room was very quiet until Judith cried out: "I've never cheated! Honestly, I haven't! I would never do such a thing!"

The class waited. What would the Rabbi do now?

At last he began to speak. "Judy, I'm not accusing you, or any other member of the class. I don't think I'm going to accuse Jonathan either. Perhaps I'm the guilty one. Perhaps I should accuse myself."

"But, Rabbi!" Sarah interrupted. "You haven't copied. You haven't cheated!"

Rabbi Mayer answered quietly, "No, I haven't copied and I haven't cheated. But in a sense I am guilty of something else. I have tried to teach you the facts of Jewish history, Jewish literature, and Jewish ceremonies. But I have failed to impress you with the purpose of Jewish history, literature, and ceremonies. I have been guilty of neglect. I have neglected the mystery of the Still, Small Voice."

The class was puzzled. What did the Rabbi mean by the Still, Small Voice? What was the mystery? What did it have to do with cheating? Whose voice was it? Why was it so important, and what did it say?

The Rabbi continued: "We cannot understand the real purpose of Judaism unless we hear that Voice. We cannot understand what it means to be a good Jew, a complete Jew, until we obey that Voice. We cannot live up to the ideals of our Jewish faith and apply those ideals to our lives today unless we listen to that Voice."

Joseph asked: "But Rabbi, what *is* the Still, Small Voice, and what does it have to do with being a good Jew?"

"That is the mystery we must solve," said Rabbi Mayer. "For the rest of the year we are going to look for the answer in the Bible, the Midrash, and the Talmud. We are going to explore the teachings of Judaism, those of yesterday and today. We will learn why Judaism is a way of life, and what we must know and do to hear and obey the Still, Small Voice.

"After we have found the answer to the mystery of that Voice, perhaps we will learn why those who cheat are not good Jews, no matter how many ceremonies they observe or how many prayers they repeat. To be a good Jew means more than learning Jewish history and Jewish literature. That is why I want all of you to tear up your test papers and throw them in the wastebasket. Then we will be ready to open our Bibles to I Kings, Chapter 19, Verses 11–12, and begin our search for clues to the mystery of the Still, Small Voice."

What Is a "Good" Jew?

You see, that's how it all began. The class was somewhat bewildered and considerably relieved. The students tore up their test papers, threw them in the wastebasket, and returned to their seats. Everyone was eager to discover the secret of the mysterious Voice. While David was leafing through the Bible looking for the First

Book of Kings, he whispered to Shoshana that he thought it had something to do with "conscience" and "the right way to act." Shoshana started to answer, "it's being good," but Rabbi Mayer cleared his throat and began speaking. He said: "The Still, Small Voice teaches us that Judaism is a way of life, and therefore a good Jew is one who. . . ."

CHECKING UP ON YOUR OWN OPINION

Choose the four most significant definitions of a good Jew. Decide on the order of their importance and discuss them in class.

A Good Jew is One Who:

Attends religious services and observes Jewish customs and ceremonies.

Is kind, considerate, and righteous in his dealings with others, and is devoted to his temple or synagogue.

Is interested in community activities and works for the Red Cross, Community Chest, etc.

Works for and contributes to the United Jewish Appeal and other Jewish charities.

Promotes goodwill and interfaith activities for Christian-Jewish understanding.

Is active in the Zionist Organization or Hadassah, and works in behalf of the State of Israel.

Belongs to organizations such as B'nai B'rith, the National Council of Jewish Women, etc.

Rarely attends religious school or religious services but defends Jews whenever they are insulted.

Observes Jewish traditions such as the lighting of candles on the Sabbath, Kiddush, and a Passover Seder in the home, but rarely attends religious services.

Is kind, considerate, and righteous in his dealings with others, but does not attend religious services.

WHAT ARE YOUR REACTIONS?

List the first things that come into your mind as you look at this word: JEW.

Suppose someone says to you, "You don't look like a Jew!" What are your feelings? Have you been complimented or insulted?

Suppose someone says to you, "You don't look like an American!" How would you feel about this? Would you consider this a compliment or an insult?

What would a Christian think of when he sees the word "Christian"?

When a Jew uses the word "Jew" or "Jewish," does he think of: Ten Commandments, goodness, God, holiness, kindness, mercy, truth, justice, service to mankind, courage?
If not, with what does he identify "Jew" or "Jewish"?

What would a rabbi think of when he hears the word "Judaism"? List those things that will come into his mind.

Are most Jews proud of being Jewish? Are you? Give the reasons for your answer.

READ AND DISCUSS IN CLASS

Donald, David, Jonathan, Shoshana, and Judith believe themselves to be good Jews. Which one listens to the Still, Small Voice? What do you think?

The Case of Donald B.

Donald B. doesn't attend religious school. He could have been confirmed last year, but he dropped out of class because it interfered with football practice. His parents urged him to return to school, but Donald insisted stubbornly that he was a good Jew without going to religious school. He never attends religious services, and thinks that Jewish ceremonies and festivals have no significance.

When the United Jewish Appeal Campaign was held in his community, Donald took a very active part. He volunteered to head the Youth Division. He contributed generously from his own earnings and worked hard toward reaching the quota set for the Youth Division. Through his leadership, effort, and hard work, the quota was reached.

The Case of David R.

David R. attends religious school because his parents are very active in the temple and they think he should have a Jewish education. Dave isn't so sure. He is always too busy to participate in religious school programs, and he refused to do any work for the United Jewish Appeal. He made a small contribution, but not out of his own earnings or allowance. His father gave him the money. When his family gets together for Jewish holydays and festival observances, Dave always manages to have a Boy Scout meeting to attend, or he has to get away early to study with a friend. Mrs. R. says that she has stopped asking Dave to attend Friday evening services with the family.

Dave won the boxing intramural contest for his class. Recently, he was called into the principal's office for fighting. He refused to say he was sorry for hitting an older student, because the other fellow had made some insulting remarks about Jews. Dave refused to "take it." He said that he was a Jew and proud of it, and that he would fight anyone who insulted his religion or picked on someone because of the color of his skin. Dave made quite a scene about six months ago when he waded into a group of bullies tormenting a Negro boy. Dave says that anti-Semitism is un-American. He started a club of Jewish students to study the problem of anti-

Semitism, and to take steps to fight bigotry in his school and neighborhood.

The Case of Jonathan G.

Jonathan's classmates think he is a little peculiar because he is so very religious. He says prayers upon rising and going to bed. He never tastes a morsel of food without pronouncing the proper blessing. He recites Kiddush on Friday evenings, and attends Sabbath services regularly. On the High Holydays, Jonny assists the Rabbi in conducting the Children's Services, and reads the portion from the Torah. His parents are very proud of him and his devotion to Jewish ritual.

There are some things about Jonny, however, that his parents don't know. He will cheat on examinations, and he has an agreement with two of the brightest students in his class to copy their workbooks and papers. However, he claims to be the most religious boy in school, and points with pride to the fact that he can say a Hebrew blessing faster and more accurately than any of his classmates.

After services one Friday, he went out with a group of boys and had a lot of fun letting the air out of a neighbor's tires. His conscience bothered him a little, but he said a special prayer to God and felt assured of forgiveness. After the prayer, he chuckled to himself at the thought of the neighbor's irritation when he discovered that all four tires on his car were flat. Jonny always has to have his own way, and doesn't care how much he hurts the feelings of others. He likes to use words like "dirty nigger" to colored boys smaller than himself. He was scheduled to participate in a special Youth Service at the temple, and speak on "The Responsibilities of Jewish Youth," until that embarrassing incident in class.

The Case of Shoshana M.

Shoshana is an enthusiastic leader of a Young Judaea Club. Her parents have been loyal and hard-working Zionists for many years. She is a brilliant student, but isn't particularly interested in anything Jewish unless it relates to Zionism. She knows all the favorite Israeli songs and dances. Shoshana rarely attends any religious services unless the Rabbi speaks on Zionism. She says she wants to go to Israel and live in a collective colony called a Kibbutz. She was among the first to volunteer for the drives to collect money for displaced Jews in Europe. She collects money for the Jewish National Fund and saves her pennies for the Blue and White boxes in her home. Often she deprives herself of candy or a good movie to save money to buy land in Israel. Shoshana says that anti-Semitism may

come here just as as it came to Germany. She insists that Israel is
the only safe place for Jews.

Shoshana speaks Hebrew with ease, and loves to memorize the
works of the great Hebrew poet Bialik. However, when she was
asked to read part of the Hebrew portion of a Friday evening service, she managed to get out of it by saying that she had to take care
of her little brother that night. Recently Shoshana was awarded a
scholarship to a Zionist Youth Camp because of her leadership in
the Young Judea Club.

The Case of Judith K.

Judith is regarded as a model citizen in her public school, co-
operative and helpful in every way. She is horrified at the idea of
cheating, and she has never been known to tell a lie. She is kind-
hearted and goes out of her way to help people. Sometimes her
parents are annoyed because she neglects her studies to take care of
every stray dog and cat in the neighborhood. Judith say she is
going to devote her life to "doing good." She doesn't find her
studies in Judaism very interesting. She says that she can be good
and do good without being religious. She thinks it is more important
to do kind deeds than to do religious school assignments. She doesn't
belong to any Jewish organization or club because she feels that too
much time is wasted in talk. When the Youth Division of the
United Jewish Appeal was organized, Judith said that helping Jews
alone was selfish. She wouldn't participate in any Zionist organization, but she did give some money to help the people of the State
of Israel. She insisted that there were other people who needed help
too, and she didn't think that giving a lot of money to Israel was
fair to all the others, such as the poor Chinese, the Greeks and the
Mexicans. Instead of giving some of her money to the United
Jewish Appeal, she divided it among many organizations helping
many needy people. A minister in her neighborhood heard about

this and preached a sermon praising Judith for her kindness and her good Jewish heart. Judith spends every Saturday afternoon at the Methodist Home for the Aged, running errands, and reading to the residents.

Now you know a good deal about Donald, David, Jonathan, Shoshana, and Judith. Which one is a good Jew? Which one obeys the Still, Small Voice?

Suppose we return to the classroom and listen to Rabbi Mayer's comments about what it means to be a good Jew.

The Splinter of the Bat

"Some of you have the idea that Judaism is for grownups only, that it doesn't have much to do with young people. That is a mistaken idea," said Rabbi Mayer. "The Still, Small Voice can speak to you. The teachings of Judaism are meant for you. The practice of Judaism is meant for you. Judaism is to be used every day of your life—and what's more, a good Jew doesn't think of Judaism as a splinter of the bat.

"This puzzles you, doesn't it? Let me give you an example.

"Suppose you take a sturdy baseball bat, remove a splinter of wood from it, and then try to hit a home run with the splinter. A splinter of a bat is only part of the bat, and anyone knows that you can't hit a home run with a splinter. You need the whole bat.

"And so it is with Judaism. It is made up of many different parts. Some people take only one aspect, one part, one splinter of Judaism, and think they are good Jews.

"To solve the mystery of the Still, Small Voice, to discover what it means to be a good Jew, we must find out how to use *all* of Judaism as a way of life. We must never select just one aspect as a splinter of the bat."

Rabbi Mayer spoke rapidly:

Judaism is not a prayerbook!

Judaism is not a history!

Judaism is not the Bible alone, the Talmud alone, or any one book!

Judaism is not the Synagogue alone, or the Holy Ark, or the Eternal Light alone!

Judaism is not just attending Religious Services, or observing Holydays and Festivals!

Judaism is not just giving money to charity, or fighting anti-Semitism, or helping a good cause!

Judaism is not just being kind, unselfish and truthful!

Judaism is not a single act of ritual or a single belief!

BUT

Judaism is all of these put together!

Judaism is a way of life! Your life!

Judaism is your hopes, your dreams, your speech, your thoughts!

Judaism is the way you act at home, in school, in the temple, on the basketball floor!

Judaism is how you feel and act toward your fellow students!

Judaism is a guide to help you choose between good and evil, right and wrong!

Judaism is a holy, religious way of life!

Jonathan burst out. "Is that what it teaches in the *V'ohavto,* 'Thou shalt love the Lord thy God'? I mean, when it says we should follow Judaism 'when thou sittest in thy house, when thou walkest by the way, when thou liest down, and when thou risest up'? That Judaism is with us all the time and should be practiced and used every day and night of our lives?"

"Right, Jonathan, right," said Rabbi Mayer.

Joseph's hand went up. "But Rabbi, what makes these things Jewish? Can't someone be decent and good without being Jewish? What is Jewish about this way of life?"

Rabbi Mayer smiled. "Those are good questions, Joseph, but I can't answer them as Hillel did, standing on one foot. Let's wait until we find out more about the Still, Small Voice.

"Sarah, what is your question?"

"Would you describe a good Jew about our own age, someone who listens to the Still, Small Voice?" asked Sarah. "What I mean is, someone who doesn't use Judaism as a splinter of the bat?"

"Yes, Sarah. Let me tell you about someone your own age. His name is Joel."

Joel Lives By His Faith

Joel doesn't hit the ball with a splinter of the bat. He uses the whole bat. He likes sports and public school activities and participates in them. He is enthusiastic and eager about his religious school studies. He takes pride in the heroes of his faith; he treasures the wisdom, the courage, and the holiness of the prophets, rabbis, and teachers. He attends services regularly. He observes Jewish ceremonies and customs not because he has to, but rather because he loves their meaning and beauty. He is vitally concerned with the welfare of his people in all lands, and when he is called upon to work for the United Jewish Appeal, he does so to the best of his ability. He knows the blessings and the prayers of his faith, and they are uttered with great sincerity on his lips. Joel does everything he can to promote the welfare of the State of Israel and its people, and contributes his earnings generously. He believes in America, his own country, and wants to help build a vital, living Judaism in America that will make his country stronger. No one can insult Jews in Joel's presence and get away with it. He is proud of his faith and his people. Just as he speaks of the religion of his non-Jewish friends with respect, so he insists that Judaism must be spoken of with respect. Joel is convinced that a good Jew must be just, merciful and upright in his dealings with others. He says he cannot be a good Jew unless he is a good, honorable, and righteous man. Once he heard his rabbi preach a sermon using the text from the prophet: *The righteous shall live by his faith.* To Joel, that is one of the most important verses in the Bible.

"Does that answer your question, Sarah? If not, we will discuss it further the next time we meet. We have only started our search. Next week we will try to discover some new clues to the mystery of the Still, Small Voice. Until then, class is dismissed."

QUESTIONS FOR DISCUSSION

1 Now that you have read about Donald, David, Jonathan, Shoshana and Judith, go over your definitions of a good Jew. What changes will you make in the order of importance?

2 What do you think of this statement: "Anyone who cheats is not a good Jew, no matter how much Jewish history he masters, and no matter how many Jewish ceremonies he may observe."

3 What is the meaning of "conscience"? Is it the Still, Small Voice within us? How can the "Voice" help us to be more than a splinter of a bat?

4 Give some examples of how Judaism can be applied at home, in public school, in your relationships with your friends and classmates.

5 Give examples of how Judaism can be applied in sports.

6 What do you think Rabbi Leo Baeck meant by this statement: "A Jew without religion is an incomplete man. Perhaps a Gentile, too, without religion is incomplete; but a Jew without religion is surely an incomplete being. Be complete! That is my advice. Stop being incomplete!"

7   Rabbi Mayer's class was scheduled to conduct a Friday evening service. In view of the cheating episode, do you think the class should conduct the service?

8   Look up the dictionary meaning of *Ethics* and *Morality*. What do these two words have to do with religion?

GOING TO BAT FOR JUDAISM

Here is a drawing of a baseball bat. Copy it, and show how the bat of Judaism is constructed.

Place a number in each section of the bat to show the requirements of a good Jew—the most important in the largest section, the next most important in the next largest, etc.

1   Observing Jewish ceremonies
2   Attending religious services
3   Helping Jews in need
4   Helping Christians in need
5   Being kind, just, and honorable at all times
6   Belonging to Jewish organizations
7   Combating anti-Semitism

THINGS TO DO

1   Pretend you are a Jewish newspaper reporter. Interview your parents, your brothers and sisters, and a professional worker, such as the Director of the Jewish Welfare Fund or the Jewish Social Service Bureau. Ask this question, "What is a good Jew?" Report at the next session of the class.

2   According to the rabbis, "the voice of Jacob" means religious wisdom, and "the hands of Esau" represent physical, material might.

Write an essay on the modern interpretation of the verse, Genesis

27:22: *The voice is the voice of Jacob, but the hands are the hands of Esau.* Explain what "the voice of Jacob" means today, and what it says about the problems of prejudice, injustice, and war. Give examples of unworthy deeds that might be performed by "the hands of Esau." Give examples of how "the voice of Jacob" might help you make wise decisions.

SELECTED QUOTATIONS

What Is Judaism?

Judaism is the sum total of Jewish experience, of Jewish living, hoping, planning, suffering. It includes the past and the present, the old traditions and the present system of ethics. It is a religion and a guide, a culture and a philosophy, a moral system and a means of salvation. But most important of all, it is a way of life. It is the Jewish way of finding God, and of seeking perfection in man. It is, indeed, the textbook and the spiritual constitution for the Jew.

RABBI ALEXANDER A. STEINBACH,
What Is Judaism?

Communion With God

Judaism seeks to extend the concept of right and wrong to every aspect of behavior. Jewish rules of conduct apply not merely to worship, ceremonial, and justice between man and man, but also to such matters as philanthropy, personal friendships and kindnesses, intellectual pursuits, artistic creation, courtesy, the preservation of health, and the care of the diet.

RABBI LOUIS FINKELSTEIN

The Good Way

Here is the opportunity to make a Jewish life that is not just one of organizations, but the good way of every Jew. Now is the time to make Jewish religion paramount in Jewish life—that is, Jewish religion as a way of life, as a road up the mountain side—a path of living by which every Jew may reach the high elevation that is our ethical teaching.

Editorial, the B'nai B'rith *National Jewish Monthly*

The Voice of Jacob

"The voice is the voice of Jacob, and the hands are the hands of Esau." (Gen. 27:22)

Said Rabbi Berachia: "When the voice of the Jews is occupied with profane learning or complaints, the hands of Esau are strong against them. But when the voice of the Jews utter words of Torah and prayer, the hands of Esau have no power against them."

Bereshis Rabba

SUGGESTED READINGS

Enelow, H. C., *The Faith of Israel*, Lesson XII.
Feldman, Abraham, *The American Jew*.
Joseph, Morris, *Judaism As Creed and Life*, Chapter I.
Levinger, Elma E. and Lee J., *Folk and Faith*, Part II, "The Good Life."
Steinbach, Alexander A., *What Is Judaism?*, Chapter IX.

THE VOICE OF GOD

Is God A Magician?

Marco and his Tricks

The night before the class met again, the Men's Club of the Temple sponsored the annual Father, Sons, and Daughters Banquet. By popular request, Marco the Magician was there to entertain with his remarkable tricks. Marco had a running line of patter to accompany his deft sleight-of-hand maneuvers, and his performance was an amazing and mystifying exhibition of talent. This year Michael and Bernard vowed to learn the magician's secrets. They found front-row seats where they could observe him closely.

When Marco called for an assistant to take part in one act, Michael volunteered quickly, hoping to discover the solution of the trick. He returned to his seat a little later, shaking his head in complete bewilderment. Marco had taken a compact and lipstick from Michael's pocket, pulled a pink ribbon from his hair, and removed a package of bobby pins from his wallet, while the audience roared with laughter.

When the students met for class the next day, everyone began talking about Marco the Magician. After the roll was called, Bernard asked: "What did you think of the program last night, Rabbi? Did you enjoy the magic?"

The Master Magician

"I thought the program was excellent, Bernard," said Rabbi Mayer, "and I thoroughly enjoyed the magic. As a matter of fact, magic is what I want to talk about today. Before Judaism became a way of life, it was concerned with magic, just like the other early religions. God was believed to be the Master Magician, and He ruled the world with a heavenly bag of tricks.

"You look surprised. Well, a long time ago, religion had very little to do with a good and just way of life. Religions were based on magic. Men worshipped God because they were impressed with His magic. They wanted Him to use His heavenly bag of tricks to help them. You laughed at the magician last night. You were entertained by his tricks. In early times, men were terrified of God the Magician, and people trembled with fear at the thought of His magical powers.

"You see, people knew very little about the workings of the universe. The wonders of nature, the wind, the rain, even the crops of the field seemed to them to be the results of magic. In their ignorance, men thought that when God was angry, He waved a wand and the heavens flashed with jagged streaks of fire. His magic rumbled forth in booming, ear-splitting volumes of sound when He was displeased. When the crops flourished and there was food for all, it was because of God's magic. When there were plagues and famine and the people died of starvation and disease, that too was God's magic, their punishment for having angered Him.

"After the program last night, the Chairman of the Entertainment Committee gave Marco a check for his performance. Primitive peoples paid their Divine Magician, too. They tried to bribe Him and coax Him into being friendly and helpful by giving Him sacrifices and offerings. Their special words of praise were called prayers and incantations. Those who were believed to be favorites of the Magician, those who knew how to please Him, were called shamans, medicine men, and priests.

"This was the religion of the primitive man—before Judaism developed. It had nothing to do with religion as a way of life. It had nothing to do with justice or truth, mercy or righteousness.

"It had nothing to do with the way a man treated his neighbors or his family. It had nothing to do with the mystery of the Still, Small Voice. Religion was magic, and God was a powerful magician who demanded endless sacrifice of food and beasts to satisfy His hunger."

WHAT DO YOU THINK?

1 What is the difference between religion and magic?

2 The dictionary definition of magic is ___
The definition of religion is ___
How do we confuse these two words?

3 In what way do we still think of God as a magician today?

4 We no longer offer sacrifices, but how do we use prayer as a form of magic today?

5 Give an example of a prayer that asks God to perform magic.

6 How do we attempt to bribe God to perform magic for us today?

7 If a man wants God to do something for him and he offers to pay a large sum of money to the synagogue or to charity, is this an attempt to bribe a God of Magic? Do you think God will be influenced by the gift?

8 Look up the passages in Leviticus 10:1–2; Leviticus 20:6; Joshua 10:12–14; Second Kings 4:2–7. Is this magic? What do you think?

A New Idea of God

Rabbi Mayer continued the lesson. "It took a long time, but the teachers and leaders of the Jewish people were the first to proclaim a new concept of God and a new idea of religion. They said that God was not a magician who played tricks on man. They insisted that religion was not magic, and that God did not want meaningless sacrifices. The Holy God, the Ruler of the universe, the Father of all men, wanted justice. He loved righteousness more than burnt-offerings. He delighted in truth and mercy. Here was a startling new idea of God, a God who was vitally concerned with the way man acts, the way he treats his neighbors and his family.

"People didn't want to give up their magic and think of God in this new way. They fought those who taught this new idea, but the teachers and prophets of Israel were not easily shaken. They taught with stubborn faith that religion is not magic, and that God is not a magician. Religion is a way of life, they said, and the Holy God, the Divine Father of all, demands truth and holiness from those who worship Him. They believed that God was not in the wind, or in an earthquake, or in the fires of sacrifice—but in the Still, Small Voice that summoned men to deeds of justice and mercy.

The Young Abraham

"When Abraham, the father of the Jewish people, was young, most people believed in spirits and many gods. They bowed down before idols of stone and wood. Abraham believed in one God, and smashed the idols in his father's shop. Still he clung to his old belief in a heavenly magician. So he challenged God to prove His power. He took a heifer, a goat, a ram, a turtle dove and a young pigeon, divided them and set them down opposite each other. And then the Bible tells us, in Genesis 15:17:

> *And it came to pass that when the sun went down, and there was thick darkness, behold a smoking furnace and a flaming torch that passed between these pieces.*

"The sacrifices were consumed by fire, and Abraham believed in the power of God's magic. But this was not the true worship of the one God. This was not the echo of the Still, Small Voice. God did not want Abraham to think of Him as a Magician who demanded sacrifices and offerings. God wanted Abraham to believe in Him as a God of mercy and justice. Many years later, the way Abraham tried to prevent the destruction of the wicked cities of Sodom and Gomorrah proved that at last he had heard the Still, Small Voice."

The Wicked Cities

Sylvia raised her hand, and said: "I've always wondered why those two cities were destroyed. Fire rained down on them from heaven, didn't it?"

Rabbi Mayer answered. "Yes, the Bible tells us that brimstone and fire rained down upon Sodom and Gomorrah, 'and the smoke of the land went up as the smoke of a furnace.' God was very angry with the people of these cities because they were cruel and brutal, selfish and unjust. Notice how this shows a change in people's idea of God. Once people thought that God would be angry if sacrifices were not offered to Him. It did not matter whether people were cruel or unjust. But the God who appeared before Abraham was not a God of magic. He did not want sacrifices. He did not want praise. He wanted people to be kind and just, not only to each other, their families and friends, but even to strangers. Now this may not sound odd to us. But in Abraham's time, it was strange indeed to think that God was interested in kindness, mercy and justice.

"A few minutes ago, Sylvia asked why God would want to punish the inhabitants of Sodom and Gomorrah. The sages and teachers of Judaism asked the very same question themselves. Here is one answer.

The Bed of Torture

"God was very angry with Sodom and Gomorrah because their inhabitants were unbelievably cruel. When a stranger came to town, they starved him. But they gave him bags of gold and many jewels. After the stranger died of starvation, they congratulated themselves on their cleverness as they took the gold and jewels away from him.

"And when a stranger appeared, they put him in a bed they had placed in the town square. If he was too short for the bed, they would stretch and pull his legs and body until he was the length of the bed. If he was too long for the bed, they cut off his legs to fit him into it. They delighted in torture and the suffering of their victims.

"There is a lesson behind this story of the torture of strangers. The people of Sodom and Gomorrah insisted that everyone think as they did, and act as they did. There could be no differences in Sodom and Gomorrah—no differences of worship, or belief, or action. According to the rabbis, this is why the cities were doomed to destruction.

"You probably agree that these cities deserved their fate. Yet Abraham tried to save them. Even though they were his enemies, even though they were cruel and evil, Abraham pleaded for them.

How Abraham Grew Up

"Abraham believed that God was just and merciful. When he heard that Sodom and Gomorrah were to be destroyed, he appealed to God, saying,

> *Wilt Thou indeed sweep away the righteous with the wicked?*

Innocent people, good people, would be killed along with the wicked. 'Why should this be?' Abraham asked. Then he tried to bargain with God, saying, 'Suppose there are fifty righteous people in the city. Would You not withhold destruction for their sake? O God, how can You kill the fifty righteous with the wicked? Is this justice?

> *Shall not the Judge of all the earth do justly?*

"And God agreed that if there were fifty righteous people in the cities, He would spare all the rest for their sake. But fifty righteous people could not be found.

"Abraham was afraid, but again he appealed to God. 'If there are forty-five righteous people, will You destroy the city?' And God heeded him again. But forty-five righteous people could not be found. Abraham continued to plead with God. And God said that even if there were only ten righteous people, for their sake He would not destroy the rest. But in all of Sodom and Gomorrah, there were not ten righteous people, and so the cities were destroyed forever.

"Believing in a God of mercy, Abraham knew that he must be merciful, even to his enemies, even to the inhabitants of the wicked cities. Believing in a God of justice, Abraham knew that he must be just. He did not merely *say*, 'I believe in God, a God who is merciful and just.' Through his actions, he showed that he heard the Still, Small Voice and that he truly believed in a God of mercy and justice.

The Challenge

"Have you ever proved your love of God? It is very easy for us to say we love God, but it is very hard to prove that love.

"The Bible tells us that God decided to test Abraham's love. He commanded Abraham to take his only son, Isaac, to Mount Moriah, and there to offer him up as a sacrifice. Abraham brought his son to the mountain top, and prepared the wood for a burnt offering. As he took his knife in hand, an angel of the Lord called to him and commanded him to let the boy live.

"Now God knew that Abraham had met the test. He was willing to sacrifice his son to show his obedience to God. But God did not want this sacrifice. Abraham was told to sacrifice a ram in place of his son.

"This story is a very important one. It tells us that the Jewish people were among the first to protest against human sacrifice to a God of magic. It told the people of that time that there were other, better ways to show their love for and obedience to God.

"Imagine how superstitious and primitive people were in those days! They believed that God demanded human sacrifice. It took great faith and courage for Abraham to meet this test, to offer his beloved son to show his love for God. His faith was rewarded. And this was the beginning of a new concept in the history of mankind. Not human sacrifice, but justice and mercy, was God's requirement for all people.

Modern Magic

"For many years after the death of Abraham, people still believed in a God of magic. Do you remember the story of the ten plagues, and how the children of Israel were delivered from bondage in Egypt? This was a God of magic Who performed wonders and miracles to help His people. Do you remember the story of Aaron in the Book of Exodus? He waved a magic rod over all the rivers, streams, pools and ponds of Egypt, and they turned to blood. But the magicians of Egypt had secret arts, the story says, and used them, and Pharaoh's heart was hardened. Both Aaron and the magicians of Egypt stretched forth their hands, and there was a plague of frogs. They brought forth the plagues of gnats and flies, diseases of cattle, boils, pestilence, hail, darkness, and the slaying of the first-born of the Egyptians.

"This story was written very early in the history of the Jewish religion. It describes a God of magic, secret arts, and miracles. Even to this day, some people still think of God as a super-magician. They believe that priests, ministers, and rabbis help God perform magic through prayers and ritual. To them, God has very little to do with the ideals of truth, justice, and mercy.

"That is why it is so important for us to understand the mystery of the Still, Small Voice. That is why it is so important for us to learn how the teachers, prophets and rabbis took the deception of magic out of religion, and taught about the wondrous God who performs miracles every day, in nature and in the heart of man. They taught about a God who does not rely upon a heavenly bag of tricks, but who calls upon us all to help turn evil into goodness, hate into love, wrongdoing into justice, and suffering into happiness.

"If we must have magic, then let obedience to the Still, Small Voice offer us the modern magic of religion. It can transform our world into a world of justice, where mercy rules, and where all men strive for brotherhood and peace."

Religion Grows Up

Rabbi Mayer closed his notebook. "Yes, our ancestors believed in magic. Most religions began with ideas of gods who worked unbelievable wonders. It was the genius of Judaism that changed this notion of God, and offered the world a new and holy God—a God who loves mercy, righteousness and truth."

Miriam was the first to raise her hand. She seemed puzzled as she asked, "Does this mean that Judaism had to grow up, that it changed—like being a baby and then growing into an adult?"

"You are quite right, Miriam," answered the Rabbi. "Many people believe that all of Judaism came about at one time and in one place. But that isn't true. The faith of Israel developed over a long period of time. At first it was crude and childish, and then it became wiser and more meaningful and beautiful. Magic is the baby stage of religion. It is the selfish, demanding stage of religion. As Judaism grew up, there was less and less magic. Men learned to think of the welfare of others—the sick, the poor, the old, the helpless. They learned to listen to God in the Still, Small Voice that spoke of mercy and compassion for all of God's children."

The Kindergarten God

Bernard burst forth with his question. "But Rabbi, didn't Moses use magic? I mean, the ten plagues, and freeing the Israelites from the Egyptians, and waving the magic rod? Didn't Moses believe in a God of magic, and didn't God use magic to save His people?"

"Yes, Bernard. At first Moses too worshipped a God of magic. Natural events seemed like magic in those times. This was the baby, or kindergarten age, of religion. Moses too had to grow and mature until he could hear the Still, Small Voice. Moses began to know the true God when he heard this proclamation of the Lord:

> *The Lord, the Lord God, merciful and gracious, long-suffering and abundant in goodness and truth. Keeping mercy for thousands, forgiving iniquity and transgressions.*

"But what about the burning bush, Rabbi? Wasn't it magic when Moses saw God in the burning bush?"

"Moses thought that God was like a man, and that he would see the figure of God in the burning bush. Instead, he saw the bush on fire. It burned, but it was not consumed. It did not disappear. The legend of the burning bush has a lesson: Moses could not see God, but he could feel the presence of God, and he heard God speak to him through the Still, Small Voice. This was a great step forward in his belief in God, and in the Jewish idea of God.

"The young Moses thought that God had a name, just as people have names, and he asked God to tell him His name. God gave a strange answer, saying:

I will be what I will be.

You see, Moses still thought of God as a man—a superman, a miracle-man, perhaps, but nonetheless a power with the body of a person. He asked God:

Show me, I pray Thee, Thy Glory.

He wanted God to reveal Himself. He wanted to see God's face. But God said:

Thou canst not see My face, for man shall not see Me and live.

"Moses was disappointed. Then God told him there was a way to see Him. I'm not going to tell you what God said, but I'll give you a clue to the answer: Exodus, Chapter 33, Verse 19. Write it down in your notebooks, and look it up. After you have learned how God really reveals Himself to men, you will understand the difference between the kindergarten belief in God, and a grown-up, mature belief in God."

David wanted to know, "What is the kindergarten belief in God, Rabbi?"

At first Rabbi Mayer didn't answer. Then he walked to the blackboard and picked up a piece of chalk, and said with an air of mystery, "I'm not going to tell you. That's what you are going to find out for yourselves. If you want to know what a five- or six-year-old child thinks about God, then do the following."

This is what he wrote on the blackboard:

Interview a child of five or six years of age. Ask the child to tell you what he or she believes about God. This will give you the kindergarten concept of God. Then interview an adult about his conception of God. Compare your findings, and decide whether or not most adults still have a kindergarten concept of God, and think of God as a divine magician.

What God Expects of Us

"Before you ask any more questions, let me pose one. We have been talking about what happened a long time ago. Let us bring our discussion up to our own time, to this very classroom. How many members of this class believe in a God of magic?

"Since no hands have gone up, let me ask this: How many members of this class believe in a God of truth, justice and mercy? Think before you raise your hand! Remember, if you say you believe in a God of truth, justice and mercy, it means that your God expects you to be truthful, just, and merciful in all your actions—at home, in school, at the Temple, at work, at play, on the baseball diamond, at your meetings and club activities. It means that you believe in these modern, magic, words: TRUTH—never to tell a lie, no matter how great the temptation; never to cheat on an examination, whether in public school or religious school. JUSTICE— to be fair at all times, honorable in all things; never to feel or show any prejudice toward those of a different race or religion, to those who are poorer than we are, or less educated, or less talented. MERCY —to show consideration for the weak and the oppressed; to help those who are in need; never to refuse those who look to us for support or assistance; to show kindness to the less fortunate. To love God means to love His children. To worship God means prayer, but it also means to try to live up to the ideals of God by listening to the Still, Small Voice. Now, raise your hands if you really believe in a God of truth, justice and mercy."

Every student raised his hand—except Michael. The class looked at him. He looked back at the class defiantly. "I *do* believe in God, just as you do, but it's a pretty big job to live up to these ideals, and I don't know whether I'll be able to be truthful, just, and merciful at all times, no matter how hard I try. That's why I didn't raise my hand."

Rabbi Mayer nodded in approval. "I'm glad you said that, Michael. I know it took courage not to raise your hand. It takes courage to tell the truth. But when you tell the truth, it shows that you really believe in a God of truth. Perhaps you will never be able to live up to all these ideals, Michael, but I know that you will try. That is most important. Michael has come closest to understanding the real meaning of the word TRUTH!

"Now I want you to do something in addition to your regular assignment. Take out your notebooks, write down this statement, and then memorize it. It is from the Talmud and it shows why Judaism does not think of God as a Magician.

"God said to Moses,

> *Tell the children of Israel, My children, just as I am merciful, so shall ye be merciful, and just as I am holy, so shall ye be holy!*

HOW WOULD YOU APPLY THIS QUOTATION TO THE FOLLOWING:

1 Someone says to you, "Have a heart and let me copy your homework?" Should you be merciful and let him copy your work?

2 You are planning to spend your allowance on something you want very much. The Community Chest Drive is being conducted in your school. How much of your allowance should you give?

3 Your parents have told you to be home from a date by 11 o'clock. You stay out until after midnight, and return when your parents are asleep. The next day, they ask you what time you came in. No one will ever know if you tell a lie.

4 The cashier at the cafeteria gives you your change. A few hours later, you discover that she gave you too much money.

5 In a fit of temper, you have hurt the feelings of another person. You are sorry, but feel too stubborn to apologize.

6 Some friends ridicule the dress and appearance of a classmate. You agree with them, but hesitate to say anything. Finally, they ask what you think.

QUESTIONS FOR DISCUSSION

1 For the strangest magic of all, turn to Genesis 19:26, and read how God was thought to have the power to change people into strange shapes and forms. How would you interpret this verse? How do you think the rabbis interpreted it? (If you have difficulty, ask your rabbi how he would interpret the magic described.)

2 In what way do we think of God as the young Abraham did?

3 Abraham showed that he believed in a God of justice and mercy by pleading for the inhabitants of Sodom and Gomorrah. How can we show our belief in a God of justice and mercy today?

4 According to the legend, if ten righteous people had been found in Sodom and Gomorrah, the cities would have been spared. Can you give any other examples of how the few could have saved the many?

5 The wicked rulers of Sodom and Gomorrah expected everyone to think and act alike. Do some nations today feel that same way?

6 To what extent does a democracy provide the right to be different? If a nation takes away that right, is it still a democracy?

7 What do you think God meant when He gave His name as: *I will be what I will be?*

8 How can we show our love for God?

9 How does the Still, Small Voice teach us to worship God through our actions as well as our words?

10 What is the meaning of holiness? How can a boy or girl today be holy?

11 How does the belief in a God who demands truth, justice and holiness change our idea of the purpose of prayer?

12 Abraham matured and grew up to a new belief in God. Has your belief in God and religion matured and changed since you were a little child? How?

13 The Midrash tells us that "when the Egyptian hosts were drowning in the Red Sea, the angels in heaven were about to break forth into songs of jubilation. But the Holy One, blessed be He, silenced them with the words: 'My creatures are perishing, and ye are ready to sing!' God wept even for the enemies of Israel because the Egyptians were still His children." What does such a concept of God demand of us? Compare this concept with that of a God of magic.

14 Explain how God is revealed through "His goodness passing before us."

15 What modern miracles might religion perform, to change the world from what it is to what it should be?

SELECTED QUOTATIONS

How Can We Love God?

An old rabbi centuries ago asked the question, "We are told thou shalt love the Lord thy God with all thy heart, with all thy soul, and with all thy might. How can we love God when we cannot see Him? He is the invisible Spirit, the intangible Mind of the Universe." And the answer to the question was: "We can love God best by loving His letters best! . . . How does a child learn the alphabet? He learns one letter at a time — A, B, C, D, E, — and then he combines the letters into words, and then the words into sentences, and, finally, he can read a book." That ancient rabbi said: "Every person is but one letter in God's book. The more letters you come to treasure, the more you can love God."

The question that comes to every human being is this: Are we treasuring or blurring the letters of God? We have succeeded in erasing the letters of God, millions of them, in the war. The challenge that comes to our generation is to learn how to treasure the letters of God in the knowledge that every human being, white, red, yellow, black, of every race and every creed, in every corner of the earth, is one equal consonant in the vocabulary of Divinity.

RABBI JOSHUA LOTH LIEBMAN

Those Who Shall Not See God

Four classes shall not see God—the scoffer, the liar, the slanderer, and the hypocrite.

The Talmud

The Best Claim To Heaven

One day, a saintly sage, Rabbi Baroka, was walking through the crowded marketplace of his town. He met Elijah, the wandering prophet of Jewish lore. "Who of all this multitude has the best claim to heaven?" asked the rabbi of his spirit companion.

The prophet pointed to a strange-looking man, a jailer. "That man yonder, because he is considerate to his prisoners, and refrains from all unnecessary cruelty. In that miniature hell over which he presides he has averted many a horror."

"And who else here is certain of eternal life?" continued the rabbi.

Elijah then pointed to two oddly-dressed fellows, clowns, who were amusing the bystanders. The rabbi's astonishment knew no bounds. "Scorn them not," explained the prophet. "It is always their wont, even when not performing for hire, to cheer the depressed and the sorrowful. Whenever they see a sufferer they join him, and by merry talk cause him to forget his grief."

The heart ennobles any calling. A jailer may surpass the sage in the true merit of life, and a jester may be first in the kingdom of heaven, if unselfishly he has diminished the sadness of human lives.

Adapted from the *Talmud, Ta'anith,* 22a

Modern Miracles

Real religion can work miracles. I am not thinking of physical miracles, but the miracle of changing a personality, of bringing about moral self-control, of urging one to cling to an ideal, to go out and do something for others.

. . . When human beings grow up, religion will express itself at its best. In fact, religion ought to help them grow up.

RABBI EDGAR F. MAGNIN

Proving Our Love of God

They who love God will do all that is right, without the hope of reward, and will forsake all that is evil, without the fear of punishment. They will also have no fear of anything, or of any person, in this or any other world, except of the Creator alone. And they will be indifferent to the praise and the blame of men in doing the will of God. They will be pure in body as well as in mind, and fly from evil deeds of all kinds. . . .

BACHYA IBN PAKUDA

THINGS TO DO

1 Look up Micah, Chapter 6, Verse 8. How would you apply that verse to your own life?

2 List, under the following headings, four examples of true worship of God and the practice of the ethical principles of Judaism.

Justice   *Mercy*   *Humility*

3 Which of the following verses describes God as: a man of war, a Judge, a Rock, a King, a Heavenly Father.

Psalm 78:35; Psalm 74:12; Malachi 2:10; Exodus 15:3; Genesis 18:25.

4 Look up the following passages in the Bible and explain what each

passage teaches us about God: Genesis 1:1; Deuteronomy 6:4; Leviticus
19:2; Isaiah 45:19; Exodus 34:6–7; Hosea 6:1–3; Malachi 2:10; Psalm
103:13.

5 The following verses, with one exception, describe a God of
magic. Which passage is the exception?

Genesis 32:25; Exodus 4:2–5; Exodus 14:21–22; Exodus 15:25;
Exodus 32:4; Leviticus 10:2; Isaiah 5:16.

6 Write an essay giving your interpretation of the verse, Deut. 4:12:
And the Lord spoke unto you out of the midst of the fire;
ye heard the voice of words, but ye saw no form, only a
voice.

Others passed that bush, but saw nothing nor heard the voice of God.
Why do you think Moses heard God speak? How does God speak to
us with a voice?

7   *Magician's Hat*   *Torah*

List the magic that can come out   List the modern magic that can
of this: come out of this:

SUGGESTED READINGS

Feuer and Glazer, *The Jew and his Religion*, Chapter II.
Ginzberg, Louis, *The Legends of the Jews*, Vol. I, p. 245–257.
Levinger, Elma E. and Lee J., *Folk and Faith*, Chapter XIII.
Steinbach, Alexander A., *What is Judaism?*, Chapter I.
Steinberg, Milton, *Basic Judaism*, Chapter IV.

3

THE VOICE OF THE TORAH

Ethics of Jewish Law

Mr. District Attorney

"Did any of you see the mystery on the *Mr. District Attorney* television program last night?" asked Daniel. "The court trial certainly was exciting."

Marilyn looked up from her workbook paper and said: "I don't know why you waste your time with those programs. The detective stories are all the same: killings, crime and violence. I hardly ever watch television any more because . . ."

"Maybe you don't watch television," Daniel cut in, "but your little sister told me how you sit glued to the radio, listening dreamy-eyed to those crooners singing all that stuff about love and romance

—oh boy!" Daniel let out a long mocking sigh. He looked so ridiculous that even Marilyn joined in the laughter.

Stuart sat down next to Danny. "*Mr. District Attorney* made me think that being a lawyer is exciting—you know, criminal cases and sensational trials. I had decided to study law. Then I talked to my uncle, and I changed my mind—in a hurry."

"Why, Stu? Did your uncle tell you you weren't smart enough to be a lawyer?"

Stuart gave Daniel a friendly dig in the ribs. "Quit your clowning, Danny. I'm not as dumb as all that. It's just that I thought law would be more interesting. My uncle is an attorney, and when he told me about mortgages and leases, damages, and court decisions, it all sounded as dry as dust."

"Just the sound of law makes me bored and sleepy," said Marilyn. "Why would anyone want to spend a lifetime with a bunch of wormy musty old law books?"

Rabbi Mayer had entered the classroom and was sorting papers on his desk. He heard the students talking and asked: "What's this lively discussion? Are you still talking about magic?"

"Oh, no, Rabbi," Marilyn quickly volunteered. "We were discussing *Mr. District Attorney* and the idea of becoming a lawyer. I'll bet you're glad you decided to become a Rabbi instead of a lawyer, aren't you?"

The Rabbi answered with a chuckle. "I am glad that I chose to nter the rabbinate, Marilyn. But actually, a rabbi is very much oncerned with law, Jewish law, the codes and regulations that help our people to live according to God's commandments. These laws, you know, are anything but dull. They are vital, practical guides for everyday living. The Jewish people was among the first to establish humane, kind, responsible rules for human behavior. Just as soon as everyone is here, I will tell you how the laws of the Torah added another chapter—a dramatic and magnificent chapter —to the story of the Still, Small Voice."

Proud of It

When the members of the class had taken their seats, the Rabbi began the discussion. "Very often, we hear Jews say, 'I'm a Jew and proud of it!' This is usually in answer to someone who, in ignorance or malice, has spoken unfavorably about Jews. It is right that a Jew defend his people and his faith. Still I wonder: how many of those who say 'I'm a Jew and proud of it' are really proud of being Jewish? How many really appreciate the privilege of being a member of a great and historic people? How can a person take genuine pride in being Jewish if he or she doesn't know anything about the magnificent contributions of Judaism to human thought and progress? Every time I read and study the laws and provisions of the Bible for human welfare, I am filled with pride. Remember, many of these laws were made at a time when human life was not too important. Most of the other peoples of that time were not concerned about the problems of the poor, the widow, the orphan, the sick, and the old. But to the Jew, helping the unfortunate was a command of God. It was a requirement of his religious faith. The Still, Small Voice insisted that he must help those who could not help themselves.

"We are going to open the Bible to the Book of Exodus, and read some of these ancient laws. But first, try to imagine the way people lived at that time, over three thousand years ago. There were no social agencies such as the Jewish Social Service Bureau; no homes for the aged; no hospitals; no clinics; no homes for orphan children. Widows could not support themselves by working as stenographers or salesladies. There were no pensions or social security. There were no laws to protect workingmen. There were no courts of justice or policemen to protect the people from criminals. Actually, there were few recognized laws of any kind—just certain traditions and rules of conduct that people had established for themselves.

"The Jews were among the first to establish laws of conduct and behavior. These laws were God's laws, and had to be obeyed. Those who disobeyed them would not only be punished by their rulers; they would also be punished by God.

"You may be thinking—well, if they didn't have any organizations such as hospitals and charities and orphan homes, how did they take care of those who needed help?"

WHAT DO YOU THINK?

1 How did Jewish law provide help for the old, the sick, the widow, the orphan, and the stranger?

2 Why should the study of law be interesting and challenging?

3 Is it possible for a woman to be a better lawyer than a man?

4 Why are the Five Books of Moses called "The Torah" or "The Law"?

5 It is said that the Spartans left the old and sick to perish when they could no longer work or serve. Do you think they were justified?

6 Can you sincerely say "I'm a Jew and proud of it"? If so, why are you proud of being a Jew?

7 Exodus 12:49 declares: "One law shall be to him that is homeborn, and unto the stranger that sojourneth among you." What does this mean?

8 What does the worship of God have to do with helping others?

Time in Reverse

Daniel began to daydream. He was still in the classroom, but his thoughts soared through time and space. He looked at his clothes and saw that he was wearing the tattered garments of a slave. His back was sore. Touching his burning shoulders, he felt welts formed by the taskmaster's whip. A child was crying, pleading for a morsel of food. An old man reached out a withered hand

and tried to clutch Daniel's legs. The sick lay on the ground, writhing in pain and pleading for water. Daniel reached down to help, but there were so many that he didn't know what to do first. He started to run, shouting, "Help, someone, help! Where is water? These people need food, care, medicine. Get them to a hospital before they die!" As he ran about in frantic desperation, an ugly, scarred man—he seemed to be seven feet tall—stepped in front of him. He had a sharp javelin in his hand, and he raised it menacingly, ready to strike. Daniel could almost feel the point tearing at his body. He screamed, "Police! Police!" but he remembered that there were no police! There was no law! This man was stronger and bigger than he, and Daniel knew that he was about to die. He heard voices taunting him: "So, Daniel, you think that law is dull and uninteresting?" He wanted to shout: "I'm sorry for what I said. We need law. We need rules and regulations. We need protection for those who are in need." But the words choked in his throat. His thoughts brought him back to the classroom and he heard the Rabbi's voice. "I repeat: so, Daniel, you think that law is dull and uninteresting? We'll let you begin reading from the Book of Exodus. Open your Bible to the 22nd Chapter and start with the 20th Verse."

The Book of Exodus

> *And a stranger shalt thou not wrong, neither shalt thou oppress him; for ye were strangers in the land of Egypt. Ye shall not afflict any widow, or fatherless child. If thou afflict them in any wise—for if they cry at all unto Me, I will surely hear their cry.*

"Thank you, Daniel. At that time, strangers who did not belong to the tribe or group were thought of as enemies. Yet the Israelites established rules of justice for this very stranger. The true worship

of God meant kindness to the stranger and those in need. This was a
great step forward for human society.

"Here is a religious concern with the needy, the widow, and the
orphan. God will punish those who afflict them.

"A God of justice demands justice from those who worship Him.
A God of mercy insists upon merciful laws. For an example, turn
to the 25th verse of the same chapter:

> *If thou at all take thy neighbor's garment to pledge, thou
> shalt restore it unto him by the time the sun goeth down;
> for that is his only covering, it is his garment for his skin;
> wherein shall he sleep, and it shall come to pass, when he
> crieth unto Me, that I will hear; for I am gracious.*

"I want you to remember this verse whenever you think that
religion has nothing to do with daily living, whenever you think that
religion belongs to the temple or prayers or ritual alone. This is the
purpose of religion—to help create a considerate, just, and merciful
society of men. Religion asks that men be clothed, and comfortable,
and warm. If you lend money to a man and take his clothing as
security for repayment, you must return the clothing by nightfall,
even if he doesn't pay you back. The man will need his garment to
cover himself at night.

Mercy Even for Our Enemies

"This is Judaism as a way of life—the way people lived and
worked together and acted toward one another. Mercy and consideration is shown even to our enemies:

> *If thou meet thine enemy's ox or his ass going astray, thou
> shalt surely bring it back to him again.*

"Imagine finding something that belongs to your enemy. Would
you walk past it and say, 'Let him find it himself'? Would you turn
it over to the Lost and Found? According to Jewish law, you must

return it to him yourself. It isn't easy to observe these commandments of our faith. It isn't easy to listen to the Still, Small Voice. It
isn't easy now, and it wasn't easy then.

A God of Justice

"These laws applied to all those who worshipped God. Although
God was merciful, there were limits to mercy. There were special
rules of justice for criminals and murderers.

> *He that smiteth a man, so that he dieth, shall surely be put to*
> *death.*

Now, what if someone killed a man accidentally? Was he punished
too? The God of justice is also a God of mercy, as the next verse
indicates. If the killing was the result of an accident,

> *then I will appoint thee a place whither he may flee.*

This meant that the man could escape to a city of refuge, and no
one could touch him there.

When You Borrow

"Suppose you borrowed a football, and it rolled under a truck,
and the wheels of the truck crushed the football. You would want
to have the football repaired, or buy the owner a new one. A long
time ago, if a person borrowed something and it was lost or ruined,
he did not have to do anything about replacing it—that is, until
the law in the Bible specified:

> *If a man borrow aught of his neighbor, and it be hurt, or die,*
> *the owner thereof not being with it, he shall surely make*
> *restitution.*

"In this way people were protected against the loss of their pos-
sessions."

Billy wanted to know, "Are all the laws in the Book of Exodus? Aren't there laws in the other books of the Bible?"

"Of course there are laws in other books of the Bible. The first five books of Moses are called THE LAW. Torah itself means Law, or Teaching. There are magnificent laws in the Book of Leviticus, laws that deal with personal cleanliness, purity, the rights of the stranger, kindness to animals, honesty in business—in fact, almost everything that relates to Judaism as a way of life.

The Book of Leviticus

"The Jewish people are commanded to observe the laws of purity and morality and justice. They are warned not to follow the crude, immoral, and sometimes cruel customs of the other peoples among whom they lived.

> *Ye, therefore, shall keep My statutes and Mine ordinances, and shall not do any of those abominations.*

"Let us turn to the nineteenth Chapter of the Book of Leviticus. It is called the Holiness Chapter, because of the command:

> *Ye shall be holy: for I the Lord your God am holy!*

Sandra said, "Why, that's like the lines you asked us to memorize:

> *Tell the children of Israel: My children, just as I am merciful, so shall ye be merciful, and just as I am holy, so shall ye be holy.*

"Yes, Sandra," answered Rabbi Mayer. "You see, this is one of the most important teachings of Judaism. It has a special name— ETHICAL MONOTHEISM. It means the belief in a God of truth, justice, mercy and holiness, Who demands truth, justice, mercy and holiness from those who worship Him.

"This concept is Judaism's most remarkable contribution to civilization. It is not enough to worship one God; we must worship one God of holiness who requires that His children also be holy. That is why we have holiness laws. As I read them, you will see that they are very much concerned with the practical details of life.

Religion in Action

> *Ye shall not steal, neither shall ye deal falsely, nor lie one to another. And ye shall not swear by My name falsely, so that thou profane the name of thy God: I am the Lord.*

"Think about this statement, and apply it to yourself. This is an important part of being religious. Did you ever steal anything? Wait, now: that means: Did you ever copy someone else's answers to an examination, or to a workbook assignment? Did you ever act falsely, or lie, or swear falsely? You don't have to answer these questions. Just remember God's commandments, and that if you break them, you are not truly religious.

> *Thou shalt not oppress thy neighbor, nor rob him; the wages of a hired servant shall not abide with thee all night until morning.*

"These are laws of justice, laws that have to do with the way you act and live—justice for your neighbor and for the stranger, justice for your friends, justice for your servants and your employees. Notice the concern Judaism has for the laborer. The people of Israel were commanded to give the workman his wages every day, and not delay payment. The laborer needed his wages to buy food for himself and his family.

> *Thou shalt not curse the deaf, nor put a stumbling-block before the blind, but thou shalt revere thy God: I am the Lord.*

"The handicapped deserve special consideration. Those who are maimed or crippled must be treated with kindness. It is wrong to take advantage of their physical defects.

"How remarkable it was that Judaism offered such protection to the handicapped centuries ago! How obediently the lawmakers answered the appeal of the Still, Small Voice!"

Jonathan whispered to Larry, "Have you figured out the mystery of the Still, Small Voice? Do you know what it means?" Larry didn't answer. He was listening to Rabbi Mayer.

> *Ye shall do no unrighteousness in judgment; thou shalt not respect the person of the poor; nor favor the person of the mighty; but in righteousness shalt thou judge thy neighbor.*

"Here again is the plea for justice; always judge honestly, and do not let wealth or poverty influence you. When you look at your neighbor, judge him in righteousness. Judge by his character and his deeds, and not by his wealth. In courts of justice one must not favor the poor man because of pity, nor the rich man because of his power and wealth.

"We make judgments all the time, even though we aren't judges in a court. Have you ever ignored a classmate because he or she lived in a poor neighborhood? Have you ever looked down on someone because he or she couldn't afford nice clothes, or didn't have enough money to go places with you? Have you ever voted for someone in a school election because he belonged to a wealthy family and lived in a fine neighborhood? Do you always judge your fellows with righteousness?

They Say . . .

> *Thou shalt not go up and down as a talebearer among thy people; neither shalt thou stand idly by the blood of thy neighbor; I am the Lord.*

"Don't be a talebearer, religion tells us. Don't be a gossip, spreading malicious stories about your friends and classmates. Leprosy is a horrible disease, but the rabbis say that another form of leprosy is even more terrible. Speaking evil of others, slandering others, ruining another's good name, is moral leprosy. Some people pretend that gossip is just a harmless pastime. Everyone does it, we say. But do we realize the harm it does? When you are with your friends and find yourself saying, 'Do you know what I just heard about Susan,' or 'Did you hear what Arnold did?,' remember the law:

> *Thou shalt not go up and down as a talebearer.*

Gossip and talebearing have damaged countless lives. Slander can kill! It can kill a reputation and a good name. When you are tempted to speak ill of someone, stop and think of the ruthless power of an evil tongue.

Helping the Oppressed

"Another law is very important:

> *Neither shalt thou stand idly by the blood of thy neighbor.*

What do you think this means?"

Stephen volunteered. "Doesn't it mean that if you see someone attacking your neighbor, you shouldn't just stand by and watch, but do something to help him?"

"Right, Stephen. It isn't always easy to help those who need help. Very often it takes a great deal of courage to befriend the hurt, the downtrodden, the persecuted. To be silent, or to just do nothing when a neighbor or friend needs us, is wrong."

Memories

Michael stirred uncomfortably in his seat. He remembered when some boys attacked his friend Bernard. Michael hid behind a tree until some grown-ups came along and chased the bullies away.

Ruth thought of the time her neighbor had to visit a sick sister and had asked her to baby-sit. Ruth didn't want to give up her evening. So she made some excuse to get out of it.

Joseph remembered Leonard's accident. Leonard had fallen off his bicycle onto a jagged rock, cut his forehead, and bled badly. Joseph felt so ill at the sight that he could do nothing but stand by helplessly.

The Rabbi continued: "I'm not going to enumerate all the laws of human welfare, decency, and justice. However, I want to mention one more today. Perhaps this is the most difficult of all to obey.

Vengeance

> *Thou shalt not hate thy brother in thy heart. Thou shalt not take vengeance, nor bear any grudge against the children of thy people, but thou shalt love thy neighbor as thyself: I am the Lord.*

"To resist temptation to hate, not to seek vengeance against someone who has hurt you—this takes strong character and self-control. I doubt if there is anyone in this room who has not carried a grudge at one time or another." Members of the class turned to each other, and there were smiles and nods. "It takes a big person," continued the Rabbi, "to refrain from pettiness. I can see by your smiles that you know how difficult it is to obey this law."

The Four Corners

Stuart raised his hand. "I don't want to change the subject, but when you started the discussion, Rabbi, you said that the Jews provided food for the orphan and the poor. How did they do it? Did they have free lunches, and give them charity money?"

"I'm glad you asked this, Stuart. No, there were no free lunches or charity. The Jewish principle has always been what is called *Matan B'seser*—the giving of gifts in secret. In the Holiness Chapter of Leviticus, there is a remarkable law, and this is what it commands:

> *And when ye reap the harvest of your land, thou shalt not*
> *wholly reap the corner of thy fields, neither shalt thou gather*
> *the gleaning of thy harvest. And thou shalt not glean the*
> *vineyard, neither shalt thou gather the fallen fruit of thy*
> *vineyard; thou shalt leave them for the poor and the stranger:*
> *I am the Lord your God.*

"In ancient days, many peoples thought that those who weren't strong enough or well enough to work should be left to die. Not so the Jews. It was part of their religion to take care of those in need. When land was harvested, its owner did not clear the corners of his fields. Those in need were free to come and gather the crops from the corners for themselves.

"After the harvest, the Israelites did not go over their fields again to glean what they had missed. This was left for the needy, to pick when no one could see them and embarrass them. Any fruit that had fallen in the vineyard was for the poor. No one was to go hungry.

"Today we have laws and social agencies to help the sick and the poor. A businessman doesn't have to set aside merchandise for the unfortunate. Yet the crops of the fields were as precious to the Israelites as today's merchandise is to the merchant. Not only were these valuable crops freely given; they were given according to the finest principle of charity—the free gift, in secret, to all in need.

I Am the Lord

"Have you noticed that each command to be just, considerate, ethical, and merciful ends with the words: *I am the Lord?* In this way the Jewish people were reminded that these laws were God's laws, and had to be obeyed. They were taught that God is not only in the synagogue; He is present at all times, every hour of the day. And He is concerned with what we do and how we act. Mercy and justice and help for those in need are part of the religious way of life. There can be no real religion without such requirements and such laws.

Rabbi Mayer paused, and then said, "When we study these laws carefully and think about them, we will really mean it when we say, 'I'm a Jew and proud of it.' The more we learn of Judaism and the Still, Small Voice, the more reason we have to be proud of being a Jew."

TRAFFIC LIGHTS OF JUDAISM

In an article, "The Law of Love and the Love of Law," Rabbi Robert I. Kahn, of Houston, Texas, wrote:

This is the method of Judaism. All through the ages it has set up traffic lights at life's busy corners, lights that govern men's trafficking in every walk of life—in the home, the synagogue, the market-place.

Which of the traffic lights of Judaism would you apply to the following situations: STOP, GO or CAUTION?

1 A Christian classmate has made a cutting remark about Jews. You want to retaliate with a nasty remark about Christians.

2 A new family has moved into your neighborhood. They have a child about your age. You are planning a small party with some old friends. You feel that if you invite the stranger, the party won't be as much fun.

3 You are angry with a classmate who treated you unfairly. As you leave the classroom you discover that he left his sport jacket on his chair.

4 You borrow your uncle's car to drive to the drugstore. While getting out of a narrow parking-space, you dent the fender. You return the car and the damage is not noticed. Perhaps, if you keep quiet, your uncle may think the damage occurred at another time.

5 A dance is planned at the Temple. The phone rings and a boy asks you for a date. You would rather go with another boy. Hoping that the boy you like may still call, you hesitate to accept. Yet, if you don't, you may not be invited to the dance.

6 Your grandmother is hard of hearing. She has been very irritable lately. When she chastises you for not hanging up your clothes, you want to answer back sharply. She will not be able to hear what you say to her, so what harm can there be in it?

7 Milton and Jerry are competing for the office of school treasurer. Milton has never held office. Jerry has. Milton ran for the office last year and was defeated. Your sympathy goes out to Milton because his family is not as rich as Jerry's family, and he never seems to get the breaks. You feel, however, that Jerry will make a more capable and efficient treasurer. Which one will get your vote?

8 Your crowd has gathered at your home for an evening of dancing and record-playing. The conversation turns to a discussion of a girl who is considered loud and flashy. You know something about her that will really make you the center of attention if you repeat the story. Even if you don't tell, the kids will probably hear it from someone else.

9 Old man Roxler is the "meanie" of the neighborhood. He is always complaining about the kids trampling on his lawn. He had threatened to keep the baseball the next time it landed on his lawn, and he did, the other day. It was your ball and you wanted it back. Although you were scared, you rang the doorbell and politely asked him to return it to you. Mr. Roxler refused.

10 You have a part-time job in the hardware store. A neighbor comes in and you sell him an article for 75¢. Later, you discover that the price was really 55¢. If you keep quiet, no one will ever know that you made a mistake. If you say anything, it may be very embarrassing for you to correct the mistake.

QUESTIONS FOR DISCUSSION

1 Can we be proud of the Jewish faith without a Jewish education?

2 How can we apply the Jewish command to help the stranger to

our own day? What is the attitude of most nations today toward strangers?

3 Should we help the oppressed even though they may, for example, be considered radicals?

4 The Bible commands:

Ye shall be holy, for I the Lord your God am holy!

What are the requirements of holiness? Is it possible for a young person to be holy?

5 Why do you think the rabbis compared gossip and slander to leprosy? Give examples of the damage that can be done by an evil tongue.

6 In what way has our society tolerated great injustices?

7 Does it take more courage to fight with fists than to speak out against injustice and cruelty?

8 What laws in our democracy are based on Jewish law?

9 Look up the meaning of the words "ethical" and "monotheism," and then explain how Judaism as a way of life is based on Ethical Monotheism.

SELECTED QUOTATIONS

What Does It Mean To Be a Jew?

To be a Jew means to know and preserve the great spiritual treasures for the future, to live by the rules of conduct laid down by prophet, lawgiver, psalmist and sage, to walk humbly in the presence of both God and man. To be a Jew means to be a disciple of the Torah, a lover of mankind and a worshipper of God, for it is for this, and no other reason that the Jew was created.

RABBI JOSEPH KLEIN

Moses the Lawgiver

God never gives an exalted office to a man unless He has first tested him in small things, say the rabbis. When feeding the flocks of Jethro, they tell us, Moses saw a little lamb escape from the flock, and when he followed it, he overtook it at a brook, quenching its thirst. "Had I known that thou wast thirsty, I would have taken thee in my arms and carried thee hither," he said. "As thou livest," a Heavenly Voice resounded, "thou art fit to shepherd Israel."

The Midrash

Live and Let Live

The Hebrew commonwealth was based upon the individual—a commonwealth whose ideal it was that every man should sit under his own vine and fig-tree, with none to vex him or make him afraid; a commonwealth in which none should be condemned to ceaseless toil; in which for even the bond-slave there should be hope; in which for even the beast of burden there should be rest. It is not the protection of property, but the protection of humanity, that is the aim of the Mosaic Code. Its Sabbath day and Sabbath year secure, even to the lowliest, rest and leisure. With the blasts of the jubilee trumpets the slave goes free, and a re-division of the land secures again to the poorest his fair share in the bounty of the common Creator. The reaper must leave something for the gleaner, even the ox cannot be muzzled as he treadeth the corn. Everywhere, in everything, the dominant idea is that of our homely phrase, "Live and let live."

HENRY GEORGE

Consideration for the Poor

Consideration for the poor distinguishes the Mosaic Law from all other ancient legislations, such as the Roman Law. The object of the latter seems to be primarily to safeguard the rights of the possessing classes. In the Torah, the poor man is a brother, and when in need he is to be relieved ungrudgingly not only with an open hand but with an open heart. In his noble self-defense, Job (xxxi: 17–20) protests:

Never have I eaten my morsel alone,
Without sharing it with the fatherless;
Never saw I any perish for want of clothing

But I warmed him with fleece from my lambs,
And his loins gave me their blessing.

The Rabbis continued this doctrine and declared pity to be a distinguishing trait of the Jewish character. If a Jew—they held—shows himself lacking in consideration for a fellowman in distress or suffering, we may well doubt the purity of his Jewish descent. "There is no ethical quality more characteristic of Rabbinic Judaism than *rachmonuth*— pity. The beggar whose point of view is that you are to thank him for allowing him to give you the opportunity for showing *rachmonuth*, is a characteristically Jewish figure." (Montefiore)

Commentary by RABBI J. H. HERTZ
in The Pentateuch and Haftorahs

Qualifications for Paradise

The Gates of Paradise stood open and the procession of men reached to the Heavenly Tribunal.

First came a Rabbi. "I'm learned in the Law," he said. "Night and day have I pored over the Word of God. I therefore deserve a place in Paradise."

"Just a minute!" called the Recording Angel. "First we must make an investigation. We've got to find out what was the motive of your study. Did you apply yourself to learning for its own sake? Was it for the sake of honor, or for mercenary reasons?"

Next came a saintly man. "How I fasted in the life I left behind! I observed all the six hundred and thirteen religious duties scrupulously. I bathed several times a day, and I studied the mysteries of the Zohar ceaselessly."

"Just a moment!" cried the Recording Angel. "We first have to make our investigation about the purity of your intentions."

Then an inn-keeper approached. He said simply, "My door was always open to the homeless and I fed whoever was in need and hungry."

"Open the Gates of Paradise!" cried the Recording Angel. "No investigation is needed."

NATHAN AUSUBEL, A Treasury of Jewish Folklore

If I Were a Dictator

If I were a dictator, the first book I would burn would be the Bible. I'd burn it because I'd realize that the whole concept of democracy came out of that book.

QUENTIN REYNOLDS

The True Voice of Jewish Ethics

The used-car dealer of today who turns back the speedometer, "peps up" the engine, paints the tires and employs other dishonest artifices to misrepresent his wares is a direct descendant of the decadent Romans who bequeathed to us the cynical maxim: *Caveat Emptor*, Let the buyer beware!

In other words, let the average buyer enter every store with suspicion and fear, knowing in advance that the seller is intent upon cheating and outwitting him.

Contrast this immoral attitude with Judaism's exalted laws. If the merchant overcharged on a product as little as one-sixth of its true price, the customer may return the article and claim a refund!

Short-changing, short-measuring or -weighing is distinctly forbidden. Just as deception is forbidden in cases of buying and selling, so it is prohibited with regard to hiring, contracts or money changing.

This is the true voice of Jewish ethics!

RABBI ISRAEL H. WEISFELD

THINGS TO DO

1 Look up the Code of Hammurabi. Then draw a line down the middle of a paper. Write "Code of Hammurabi" on one side of the line, and "Exodus, Chapters 21 and 22" on the other side; then compare. What are the similarities? What are the differences? Which are more humane?

2 Read through the Bill of Rights of the Constitution, and compare with the laws in Exodus 18:13–25; Exodus 22–23; Leviticus 19; Deuteronomy 17:8–10; Deuteronomy 22:1–10.

3 Look up the following verses: Ps. 71:9; Ps. 140:13; Exod. 22:20; Isaiah 3:15; Lev. 19:32; Deut. 24:17; Lev. 19:33; Exod. 23:9; Deut. 10:19; Deut. 24:10; Deut. 24:19; Exod. 22:21; Deut. 24:20; Deut. 27:19; Deut. 10:18. Decide which apply to the poor, the stranger, the widow, the orphan, the aged.

4 One of the most misunderstood passages in the Bible is the verse about "an eye for an eye." First check the following verses: Exodus 21:24; Leviticus 24:20; and Deuteronomy 19:21; then do some research to discover what the commentaries and the rabbis say about the *real* meaning of this statement. After you have completed your research, discuss in class whether or not society still applies the principle of "an eye for an eye" to present-day criminals. Here is a clue: *The Pentateuch and Haftorahs*, edited by Dr. J. H. Hertz, Volume I, Metzudah Publishers, page 405.

5 Draw up a questionnaire based on the question: "Why are you proud to be a Jew?" Distribute it to the students of the seventh and eighth grades of your Religious School. Discuss in class the answers you receive.

SUGGESTED READINGS

Cronbach, Abraham, *The Bible and Our Social Outlook*, Chs. IV, XI. \
Greenstone, J., *The Religion of Israel*. \
Steinbach, Alexander A., *What Is Judaism?* Chapters II and III. \
Steinberg, Milton, *Basic Judaism*, Chapter VIII. \
The Universal Jewish Encyclopedia, Volume 6, pp. 561 ff. \
Weisfeld, Israel H., *The Ethics of Israel*, pp. 300–314.

4

THE VOICE AT SINAI

The Tablets That Never Grow Old!

The Troopship Dorchester

"The ship's bells rang; it was one o'clock in the morning of February 2, 1943. A few moments later, a torpedo from a German submarine exploded into the troopship *Dorchester*, transporting American soldiers to Greenland. Many men were trapped, and many perished. Those who survived and were able to move fought their way out of the wreckage up to the deck as the lifeboats were lowered. Captain Greenspun issued orders to the crew: 'Abandon ship.' The winds lashed at the mangled transport. The grim-faced men on deck knew that the ship was going down, and that they would have to jump over the side and swim to the wildly bobbing liferafts. In a few more minutes it would be too late.

"Four chaplains ran among the men, urging them over the side. Each one ripped off his lifejacket and gave it to a soldier. Flares revealed the deck crowded with men struggling to find a place on the last raft. Those flares also showed something that the survivors will never forget. The four chaplains had decided to go down with the ship. They stood arm in arm, their heads bowed in fervent prayer. They were four men of God, each wearing the uniform of an officer in the United States Armed Forces. They were four men representing three different faiths, Catholic, Protestant, and Jewish: John P. Washington, a priest; Clark V. Poling and George Lansing Fox, ministers, and Alexander D. Goode, a rabbi. They were four men praying to the same God as the *Dorchester* disappeared from view and sank beneath the icy waters of the North Atlantic. May the story of the Four Chaplains be an inspiration to everyone devoted to the cause of Brotherhood."

The students of the Religious School were listening attentively as Stuart concluded his talk at the Brotherhood Week assembly. Afterwards, his classmates praised him.

"That's the best brotherhood talk I ever heard," said Miriam. "It really was wonderful," agreed Bert. "Maybe now you can answer a question for me, Stu. I know that a Christian chaplain wears a cross on his lapel, but what is the insignia of a Jewish chaplain?"

That's when the argument started. Eve Ellen said it was a six-pointed *Mogen Dovid*, star of David. Irving insisted it was a Menorah. Miriam thought it was a miniature Torah scroll. Everyone seemed to be talking at the same time. Marilyn finally raised her voice above the others and shouted: "Quiet! Rabbi Mayer was a chaplain in the war. Let's wait and ask him."

They all agreed, but the noisy debate continued.

The Jewish Chaplain

Fortunately for the other classes meeting in the temple, the Rabbi entered the room, and the noise subsided. He apologized for being late and called the class to order.

Irving immediately said: "Would you settle an argument for us, Rabbi? You were a chaplain in the war, weren't you?"

"Yes," answered the Rabbi, "but I don't see why that should start an argument."

"No, no," Irving hastily broke in. "We weren't arguing about that, but about the insignia a Jewish chaplain wears. It's a Menorah, isn't it, Rabbi?"

"No, Irving, it is not a Menorah." Irving looked surprised and disappointed. "It is the Tablets of the Law—the Ten Commandments. Every Jewish chaplain wears this emblem on his uniform. Now let's see why the Commandments are used to symbolize the Jewish faith.

"Last week we discussed Jewish laws—the rules and regulations given to the Jewish people to help them live up to the requirements of God. The Ten Commandments are laws too—the basic laws of morality, and the foundation for Jewish ethics. In fact, they are our best clue to the mystery of the Still, Small Voice."

Marilyn wanted to know, "Weren't the Ten Commandments the very first laws, laws that existed before all the others?"

"No, Marilyn," said Rabbi Mayer. "There were traditions and laws before the Ten Commandments. There were laws against stealing and murder, laws about proper conduct. But the Ten Commandments summed up the main laws of conduct, and the people were able to remember them more easily than the other laws. It took a long time, though, before they were actually written down. There were many unwritten traditions and rules, but the Ten Commandments created the greatest tradition of them all.

What Is In It?

"The Ten Commandments are also called the Decalogue, and the Tablets of the Law. They seemed very strange and startling when they were presented to the Jewish people as God's laws. You may have heard the story of how God offered the Torah to other peoples before giving it to the Jews. The Amalekites asked, 'What is in it?' And God answered, *Thou shalt not kill!* The Amalekites, who were bloodthirsty, fierce and cruel, refused to accept laws against murder. Then the Torah was offered to the Ishmaelites, who asked, 'What is in it?' And God answered, *Thou shalt not steal!* They refused to accept it, because they lived by sweeping down upon passing caravans and plundering them. And so the Torah was offered to many other tribes. But as God explained the moral laws of justice and righteousness, each refused it. When it was offered to the Jews, they gladly accepted the Torah, promising *Na-aseh v'nishma,* 'We will

58

do and we will hearken.' By accepting the Torah, they accepted the Ten Commandments and the obligation to obey them."

Commandments for Moderns

Stuart raised his hand. When the Rabbi called on him, he said a little defiantly: "These commandments are so old-fashioned. They may have been good for people who lived in ancient times, but I can't see how they apply to people today. Maybe we should have a new Ten Commandments for today—something modern and practical."

Rabbi Mayer did not seem disturbed by Stuart's comments. "Others have thought that too, Stuart," he said, "so let us examine these Ten Commandments and see whether or not they are old-fashioned. Perhaps we will decide that some of them no longer apply to our age and our lives. If so, then we will retain nine Commandments, or eight, or five—depending upon how many you think are modern and meaningful.

"To me, these are the tablets that never grow old. At the time they were adopted by the Jewish people, the Ten Commandments were considered so revolutionary and radical, so different, that other tribes and peoples thought the Jews fools to accept them. Today the Commandments are thousands of years old. Yet they are still young.

"But enough of discussion. Let us read them one by one and then we will decide whether or not they are modern, and whether or not they apply to life today. Open your Bibles to Exodus, Chapter 20, Verse 1."

WHAT DO YOU THINK?

1 Do you think that the insignia of the Ten Commandments is the most appropriate for a Jewish chaplain? If so, explain why. If not, what would be a more appropriate choice?

2 Why are the Ten Commandments the basis for Jewish ethics?

3 Both Jews and Christians revere the Ten Commandments as the foundation of the moral law. Are the Ten Commandments Jewish? Christian? Both? Explain.

4 The children of Israel accepted the Ten Commandments, saying: "We will do, and we will hearken." Why do you think they said, "We will do," before "we will hearken"? What does this have to do with Judaism as a way of life?

5 It has been said that "Judaism is a religion of deed; Christianity is a religion of creed!" Is there a difference? What is it?

The Ten Commandments

> *I. I am the Lord thy God, Who brought thee out of the land of Egypt, out of the house of bondage.*

"The Voice was heard at Sinai, as God spoke these words. He proclaims Himself as the Author of the laws. He is the God of Freedom, the One who brings deliverance from slavery. God tells the people that He hates oppression and tyranny in any form."

Billy exclaimed: "I see what that commandment means! Instead of Egypt we could use the name of any other country where the Jews were enslaved or persecuted. Later on, couldn't the people have read, 'I am the Lord thy God, who brought thee out of the land of Rome, out of the house of bondage,' or out of the land of Spain, out of the land of Russia, and during Hitler's time, out of the land of Germany, or Rumania, or Poland?"

"Splendid, Billy," smiled the Rabbi. "That's exactly it. In every age, in every land, wherever the Jews were oppressed and persecuted, they prayed to a God of freedom who would lead them out of bondage and slavery. And they were inspired with faith and courage; they were assured that deliverance was at hand. Not only were the Jews sustained with courage, but they encouraged others who were oppressed, and inspired them with faith, too.

"The First Commandment is the freedom commandment. It says that men must be free, that God insists upon liberty and deliverance from tyranny. Is that old-fashioned? Do we need that commandment today?"

The class unanimously agreed with a show of hands, and the Rabbi read the Second Commandment.

> *II. Thou shalt have no other gods before Me. Thou shalt not make unto thee a graven image, nor any manner of likeness, of anything that is in the heaven above, or that is in the earth beneath, or that is in the water under the earth; thou shalt not bow down unto them nor serve them. . . .*

"This is a very important commandment for us today. There is but one God. You know that once people made idols out of wood and bowed down before them with prayers and sacrifice. This may seem absurd to us. Yet even in recent times, people have worshipped images and false gods. Can you give me an example of how the Second Commandment was broken in Europe not too long ago?"

Sandra wasn't too sure, so she raised her hand timidly. "Didn't the people of Germany and the Nazis in other countries worship Hitler instead of God? I think the people of Japan worshipped Hirohito as a god, didn't they, Rabbi?"

"You are correct, Sandra. Yes, Hitler was worshipped as a god. He thought himself more powerful than God. Giant crowds would gather together and chant his praises. People greeted each other by saying, 'Heil Hitler.' The Nazi swastika became a kind of graven image, a symbol of might and power. Italy's Mussolini thought he was superhuman, too, and the people listened to him rather than to the God of freedom. And another country broke the Second Commandment. Joseph, do you know which one?"

"I think you mean Russia," answered Joseph. "When Stalin was in power, wasn't he a kind of god in the Soviet Union, and didn't the people believe that whatever he said was holy?"

"Yes, Joseph. Sometimes people worship ideas as gods. Sometimes they think that the State has replaced God. Whenever people forget the Second Commandment, whenever they worship men as if they were gods, they become slaves to dictators. Even modern peoples need to be reminded of the Commandment, *Thou shalt have no other gods before Me.* Then they will worship the one, true God of the universe, a God who loves mercy and justice, who despises cruelty, oppression, and slavery. When people disobey the Commandment, they eventually learn that the men and ideas they worship have taken away their freedom.

"Now: do we need the Second Commandment today?"

A chorus of "Yes" was the response to the Rabbi's question.

> *III. Thou shalt not take the name of the Lord thy God in vain; for the Lord will not hold him guiltless that taketh His name in vain.*

"When you really respect and love someone, you do not like to hear him mentioned disrespectfully. You would not use his name in a crude joke or as a curse, would you? You get angry when someone speaks ill of your best friend, don't you?

"The other day a student used the name of the football coach in an insulting ugly way. The boys on Coach Bryden's team resented it deeply. And how would you feel if someone used your mother's or father's name coarsely or disrespectfully? These little examples show how we feel when an honored name is used lightly.

"But how many times do we use the name of the Lord thoughtlessly or carelessly?

"God is holy; therefore His name is holy. As we respect His holiness, so we do not use His name in an oath or as a profane expression.

"There are some people who use the name of God to try and justify aggression or cruelty. Some people use the name of God to speak words of prejudice and hate against other races or religions. Those who say that God created the Negro as an inferior are using

God's name in vain. Those who say that God does not love those of other religions are using God's name in vain. Whenever we hear God's name in expressions of hatred, cruelty, vengeance or evil, we know that the name of God is being taken in vain.

"The Third Commandment, then, not only refers to oaths and profane expressions. It warns us not to associate God or use the name of God with anything that is not kind, noble, unselfish, and sacred.

"Whoever we are, whatever we say, there is One who hears everything our lips utter. Our voices are heard even on high. When we speak, our words should be honest and clear; our speech should be clean. When we use the name of God, it should always be with reverence and holiness."

After the class had agreed that the Third Commandment was important today, the Rabbi said: "This commandment may be even more significant than you realize. It means that when we testify in court, under oath, we are taking God's name in vain and are guilty of perjury if we don't tell the truth. And under our legal system today, perjury, or false testimony, is a crime.

"Here again you can see why these are the tablets that never grow old. The commandment against profanity or swearing, against using God's name for unworthy purposes—the commandment against false testimony—is just as important today as it was in the past.

"To prove how modern the Ten Commandments really are, we have tried to interpret three of them in modern terms. Now let's see what you can do with the remaining seven. What do you think they mean, and how would you apply them to our own times?"

LET'S SEE WHAT YOU CAN DO

IV. Remember the Sabbath Day, to keep it holy.

1 Why do we need a Sabbath, a day of rest?
2 How should we observe the Sabbath today?

3 How did the Sabbath serve the Jewish people in the past?

4 It has been suggested that since most people in the United States observe Sunday as their day of rest, the Jewish people should abolish Saturday as their Sabbath. What do you think?

V. Honor thy father and thy mother!

1 Explain what this should mean to us today.

2 The Bible states that duty toward parents is next to duty toward God. How would you interpret this?

3 What is the best way of honoring your parents?

VI. Thou shalt not murder!

1 Apply this commandment to modern life.

2 How does this commandment relate to the Jewish belief that man is created in the image of God?

3 Is it wrong to disobey this commandment at a time of war, when men are ordered to kill the enemy?

VII. Thou shalt not commit adultery!

1 What do we mean by the sanctity of marriage?

2 Judaism has always insisted upon moral character, sexual purity, and modesty of speech and actions. Why are these requirements important today?

3 When our Rabbis spoke about the purity of family life, what did they mean?

VIII. Thou shalt not steal!

1 What is meant by the sanctity of property?

2 How does this commandment apply to cheating, embezzlement, and forgery?

3 If a man steals because his wife and children are hungry, should he be punished?

4 How is this commandment disobeyed at home, in school, and in our relationships with others?

IX. *Thou shalt not bear false witness against thy neighbor!*

1 Explain how this commandment is all too often ignored today.

2 Give examples of how others may be hurt by slander, malicious gossip and false statements.

3 How is it possible for Jews and non-Jews to bear false witness against Judaism?

X. *Thou shalt not covet!*

1 What does "covet" mean?

2 Give some examples of how nations disobey this commandment.

3 How do boys and girls of your own age break this commandment?

4 How can Judaism help us to control the temptation to covet?

The Gangster and the Ten Commandments

Before Rabbi Mayer dismissed the class, he said: "I wonder what you will think about the magazine article I have before me. It is called "The Gangster and the Ten Commandments!""

"Gangster?" asked Bert. "What did he have to do with the Ten Commandments?"

"I've been wondering about the same thing," answered Rabbi Mayer. "You see, an evangelist, a traveling preacher named Billy Graham, tried to talk to a notorious hoodlum about religion. And this gangster said, 'I don't know much about religion. But I'm as religious as the next guy. I believe in the Ten Commandments!' "

The class laughed. But there wasn't even a suspicion of a smile on the Rabbi's face as he continued. "Here is a man who breaks most of the Commandments. Yet he says he is just as religious as the next man. He says he believes in the Ten Commandments. Can he be-

lieve in the Ten Commandments without practicing them? Does
he live them? Those are the real questions.

"It's easy to laugh at a gangster who makes a mockery of the
Ten Commandments. But how about other people, well-meaning
people who say they believe in the Ten Commandments, but don't
really practice them?

"Yes, we all talk about the Commandments. We profess our belief in them, we memorize them. But do we practice them and live
up to them as our code of morality? Do we observe them for ourselves in our own day—not for our ancestors at Sinai, not for the
generations of Jews who lived in the past?

"I want you to think about this most seriously, and try to find
out whether you just pay lip service to the Ten Commandments, or
whether you really try to live up to them. This is not easy. It takes
courage, character, and strong religious faith to hear the Still, Small
Voice. Don't ever think that a religious person is a weakling or a
sissy, and a hero is one who is fast with his fists or his gun. The real
hero is the man who knows how to control and conquer himself, his
faults, and his passions. That is why we need the Ten Commandments to direct us and guide us in our conduct day by day. That is
why these commandments are modern and alive. And that is why
the Tablets of the Law can never grow old."

HOW ARE YOUR BRAKES?

A member of Temple Sinai in New Orleans wrote this letter to his
grandson in another city. Read it and see how it applies to our everyday lives. Then answer the question: how can we apply the Ten Commandments as moral brakes?

> Dear _____
> . . . Can you imagine your bike without a brake? Of
> course you know what a brake is for. Among other things
> it can save you from an accident, in other words, keep you

out of trouble. But the brake cannot act by itself. When the bike is in motion . . . there is only one way to make the bike stop and that is for you to apply the brake: you, not somebody else, have to do it: you control it. It is a matter of control, is it not? And who except *you* has to use that control, or get into an accident or trouble?

And so it is with us, as human beings. The good Lord has given us brakes; not visible brakes, but mental brakes, and nobody but you can apply your mental brake, and nobody but I can apply my mental brake. So just as you have to apply your brake on your bike to keep out of an accident or trouble, so you have to apply your mental brake to keep out of trouble.

When someone is speaking and you have an impulse to interrupt, put on the brake. When someone provokes you to the point when you want to punch him in the nose, especially in school, put on the brake. When you feel that you have got to answer the teacher back, put on the brake. And what unhappiness you will save yourself, if you will not forget that God gave you a brake and use it.

It made me feel good that you did not want to disappoint me. But my dear boy, what is even more important, do not disappoint God.

With much love,   *Your Grandfather*

QUESTIONS FOR DISCUSSION

1 What is the relationship of Leviticus 25:10 and Exodus 21:5–6 to the First Commandment? What festivals dramatize the Jewish ideal of freedom?

2 Why did the Jews oppose the worship of idols? What practices were generally associated with the worship of idols? Why was Moses so outraged at the worship of the golden calf? (Read Exodus 32:15–35.) What modern idols do we worship today?

3 How do profane speech and foul language detract from Judaism as a way of life? Who is hurt when we break the Third Command-ment?

4 Are we breaking the Sabbath commandment if we go to the theatre or enjoy sports on that day? How can the Sabbath contribute to our physical and emotional health? What is meant by the statement "The Sabbath is made for man, not man for the Sabbath?"

5 The Bible asserts that to honor one's parents prolongs life. What does this mean?

6 Should the commandment against murder apply to the slaughter of animals? Is mercy killing ever justified?

7 It is said that "it pays to be good." How are we rewarded by main-taining high standards of conduct?

8 Is it stealing to cheat just a little on an income-tax return? How do adults sometimes "steal within the law"? Even though we are not prosecuted, how are we punished for stealing?

9 Is it possible to bear false witness without actually telling a lie? Give an example of a half-truth that may be as dangerous as a lie.

10 Cite examples where envy harms the envious. Is ambition a form of covetousness? Suppose someone envies the good name or the char-acter of another, and decides to acquire an equally good name and an equally fine character. Is he breaking the Tenth Commandment?

SELECTED QUOTATIONS

Amid Thunder and Lightning

Amid thunder and lightning and the sounding of the shofar, amid flames of fire that enveloped the smoking mountain, a Majestic Voice pronounced the Words which from that day to this have been the guide of conduct to mankind. That Revelation was the most remarkable event in the history of humanity. It was the birth-hour of the Religion of the Spirit, which was destined in time to illumine the souls, and order the lives, of all the children of men.

RABBI JOSEPH HERTZ

Honoring the Sabbath

A simple vegetable meal on the Sabbath in a home where there is love between husband, wife and children is better than a fatted ox in a home where there is hatred . . . Whether it be Sabbath or festival,

> *Better a dry morsel and quietness therewith,*
> *Than a house full of feasting with strife.*   *Proverbs 17:1*

And this is the meaning of the verse, "It is an honor for a man to keep aloof from strife (Prov. 20:3). One should honor the Sabbath by having no strife thereon.

JUDAH HE-HASID,
Sefer Hasidim

Respect for Parents

A young man named Dama owned a very precious stone. Some priests offered him a very large sum for it, and he agreed to sell it. He went into the next room to get the jewel, and found his father fast asleep, his feet resting on the box where the jewel was kept. Without waking his father, he returned to the priests and told them he could not sell the jewel. They then offered him twice as much for it, and then three times as much. "No," he answered them. "I would not disturb my father's rest, even if I could obtain all the treasures in the world."

The priests waited until the father awoke. When Dama brought the jewel to them, they counted out their money, the amount of the last offer they had made. But Dama refused it. He insisted on the amount of their first offer. For he did not want to profit from what he regarded as his duty in honoring his father.

The Talmud

Robbing Thy Brother

The disciples of Rabbi Simon ben Shetach bought a donkey for their teacher from an Arab. To their joy, they found a pearl on it, and they rushed back to their teacher, saying: "From now on you need not work any more, for we bought a donkey from an Arab, and a pearl was found on it."

The rabbi asked, "Does its owner know of that?" When his pupils said "No, but when we bought the donkey we also acquired everything on its back," their teacher replied: "Go, and return the pearl to him."

"But," argued the disciples, "did not Rabbi Huna say that if you find something that belongs to a heathen, you may keep it?"

Their teacher replied: "Do you think that Simon ben Shetach is a barbarian? He would prefer to hear the Arab say, 'Blessed be the God of the Jews,' than possess all the riches of the world. It is written, 'Thou shalt not oppress thy neighbor.' Now thy neighbor is as thy brother, and thy brother is as thy neighbor. Return the jewel."

The Talmud

A Kingdom of Priests and a Holy People

A snobbish lady once remarked to Rabbi Stephen S. Wise that she was a member of the Daughters of the American Revolution. "And my ancestors," said she, "witnessed the signing of the Declaration of Independence."

The rabbi replied: "That is all very well, Madam, but I would have you know that my ancestors witnessed the signing of the Ten Commandments."

Scars

As a child, I had a fiery temper which often caused me to say or do unkind things. Finally my father told me that for each thoughtless, mean thing I did, he would drive a nail into our gatepost—for each kindness, a nail would be withdrawn.

As the nails increased, getting them out became a challenge. At last, the wished-for day arrived—only one more nail. As my father withdrew it, I danced around proudly, exclaiming, "See, Daddy, the nails are all gone!"

"Yes," agreed my father thoughtfully, "the nails are gone—but the scars remain."

HAZEL FARRIS

THINGS TO DO

1 Read the full story of "The Four Chaplains." (National Jewish Welfare Board, 145 E. 32nd Street, New York, N. Y.) What does this heroic act of bravery teach us about religion as a way of life?

2 Compare the version of the Ten Commandments in Exodus 20 with that in Deuteronomy 5. List the differences.

3 Compare the version of the Ten Commandments (Exodus 20) in the Jewish Publication Society Bible with the Ten Commandments in the King James Bible. List the differences.

4 Write a paragraph showing how the Ten Commandments are the basis of the moral law for both Jews and Christians.

5 Write a brief statement on: "What I think is the most important of the Ten Commandments."

6 Debate the proposition, "Resolved: that living up to the Ten Commandments is the most important requirement of Judaism!"

7 Interview your parents, or other adults, and find out if they feel that most adults live up to the Ten Commandments today. Which Commandments are most frequently broken?

8 Write an essay giving an imaginary account of what would happen in your community if all laws were suspended for 24 hours.

9 Write an imaginary account of what the world would be like if everyone obeyed the Ten Commandments for 24 hours.

10 Compose your own version of the Ten Most Important Commandments for Jewish Youth Today.

SUGGESTED READINGS

Enelow, H. G., *The Faith of Israel*, Chapter 14.
Feuer and Glazer, *The Jew and His Religion*, Chapter 4, pp. 63–69.
The Universal Jewish Encyclopedia, Volume 3, pp. 314–315.
Thornton, Francis, *Sea of Glory* (Story of Four Chaplains).
Weisfeld, Israel H., *The Ethics of Israel*, Chapter 11.

5

THE VOICE OF THE PROPHETS

Spokesmen of God

Crystal Ball and Tea Leaves

"I don't believe that anyone can predict the future," said Gary. "How can a fortuneteller look into a crystal ball and tell what's going to happen next year or in ten years? The whole business is a fraud."

"Maybe there is something to it, something we can't understand because we're just ordinary people," Philip said as he joined in the conversation. "What about tea leaves? What about palmists, astrologers, and people who predict things by examining the bumps on your head? All sorts of strange predictions have come true."

Helaine sniffed. "You ought to have the bumps on your head examined, Philip, and as for that tea leaf reading and telling your fortune by the lines on your hand—why, that's not a bit scientific."

Henry perked up when he heard the word scientific. "Just a minute," he said. "Didn't Jules Verne predict the future and write about submarines and rocket trips to the moon a long time ago? How about H. G. Wells and some of his fantastic stories? Sure, they laughed at Edison, and the Wright brothers and . . ."

Helaine interrupted. "But that isn't the same thing. At least these men had a basis for their predictions. It wasn't just some guess pulled out of thin air."

"Say, that's a good example," said Gary. "Some scientists do pull their guesses out of thin air."

"Who? What scientists?" Helaine and Philip asked at the same time.

"Weather scientists. They send out balloons, they study air pressure, and then they guess what the weather's going to be tomorrow and even days from now. Go ahead, argue me down on that." Gary looked around triumphantly.

The group was silent for a few seconds, until Helaine spoke up insistently. "But even those weather prophets base their predictions on scientific facts. They don't have any supernatural power, and they aren't at all like fortunetellers."

Jonathan had been quiet during the discussion, busily finishing the last few lines of his workbook. Now he put down his pencil, and asked: "Don't you think the Prophets were able to predict the future either? They didn't use tea leaves, stars, crystal balls or anything else. They had the power to tell what the future was going to be like, didn't they?"

Rabbi Mayer had entered the classroom. Now he rapped on the desk. "What's this all about?" he asked. "Who's predicting what? If the class doesn't come to order, I predict that we're going to fall way behind in our work today."

"We were talking about the ability to predict the future, Rabbi," explained Jonathan. "The Prophets could tell what was going to happen in years ahead, couldn't they? Weren't they like fortune-tellers?"

Foretellers or Forthtellers

Rabbi Mayer thought a moment, and then he said: "Since you all seem interested in prophecy, suppose we think about the Prophets and their contribution to the story of the Still, Small Voice.

"A long time ago, when Samuel was Priest of Israel, people believed that the prophets were seers, men who could predict what was going to happen in the future, who could find things that had been lost. If you will open your Bibles to the Book of First Samuel, Chapter 9, you will see what I mean."

After the class had read the chapter, the Rabbi continued: "Here we see how the man of God, the Prophet, was thought of as a fore-teller. In the next chapter, Samuel tells Saul that the lost asses will be found, and that his father will be greatly concerned about him. Saul is to go to Tabor, and afterwards to the garrison of the Philistines, and when he reaches the city:

> *Thou shalt meet a band of prophets coming down from the high place with a psaltery, and a timbrel, and a pipe, and a harp, before them; and they will be prophesying. And the spirit of the Lord will come mightily upon thee, and thou shalt prophesy with them, and shalt be turned into another man.*

"The prediction of Samuel came true, and Saul prophesied with the other prophets. They traveled in groups, and acted quite differently from other men. People looked upon them with awe and fear, believing that the spirit of God in them gave them wondrous powers."

"But Rabbi," said Helaine, "I never thought of a prophet that way. It sounds more like a medicine man or a fortuneteller. I always thought the Prophets were men who preached against wickedness and injustice. Now you tell us they traveled together like an organization, and that they were a bureau of missing objects. They sound more like a lost and found department than holy men of God."

Everyone joined in the laughter. Rabbi Mayer agreed that Helaine had expressed herself very well, and amusingly. "They did sound like a lost and found department, Helaine, but all this changed. The Prophet became a spokesman of God—a forthteller rather than a foreteller. He spoke in the name of God. He poured forth wrath against injustice. He pleaded the cause of the oppressed and the weak. His voice thundered against every act of unrighteousness. The Prophets cared little about their own welfare. They defied priests, nobles and even kings, condemning them for wrongdoing and reminding them of the commandments of God. This took real courage, for kings had power over life and death. The later Prophets traveled alone, their only weapon the armor of their faith and the strength that comes from God. We cannot understand Judaism as a way of life until we understand what the Prophets taught about God and the Still, Small Voice."

Jonathan still wanted to know whether or not the Prophets could predict the future. Rabbi Mayer said he would take this up after the class discussed these questions:

WHAT DO YOU THINK?

1 Do you believe that some people can predict the future? Explain.

2 Prophecy was once a profession. What other profession started with magic and superstition, but went on to render great service to mankind?

3 Why do you think the prophets mentioned in I Samuel, Chapter 10, traveled in groups?

4 Why were the prophets concerned with justice, righteousness, and the commandments of God? What gave them the right to criticize priests, nobles, and kings?

5 Jeremiah the prophet said that he was denied the privilege of having a wife and children as other men. Why do you think he said this?

6 Some of the stories in the Bible are myths and legends. Do you think that the stories of the prophets are legends, to teach us moral lessons? Or were the prophets real men who once lived and taught? How can we find out?

7 Are there any prophets living today? Name some modern prophets. State the reasons for your choice.

8 The prophets were concerned with social justice, and the moral laws of God. Did they oppose the rituals and ceremonial practices of the Judaism of their day?

9 If the prophets described in the Bible lived today, do you think they would be Orthodox, Conservative, or Reform Jews? State your reasons.

Predicting the Future

"I'll let you try to answer Jonathan's question in a roundabout way," said the Rabbi. "He wants to know whether or not the prophets could predict the future. Suppose we give you a chance to test your own powers of prediction by analyzing the following cases."

The Case of Mr. R.

Mr. R. drinks more than he should. He has a good job, a loving wife, and fine children. Several years ago he began to associate with bad companions. They laughed at him for bringing home his paycheck and said that we only live once. In order to be a good fellow,

Mr. R. has been treating his friends to drinks and beer parties. He no longer brings home his paycheck. Mrs. R. cries herself to sleep at night because of their many unpaid bills. The children need clothes. Mr. R. pawned his wife's engagement ring to pay a fine when he was arrested for drunken driving. Mrs. R. is ashamed to invite friends into her home because she doesn't want them to be embarrassed by her husband. The doctor has advised Mr. R. to stop drinking, but he called the doctor a quack and told him to mind his own business.

What is your prediction about the future of Mr. R's job, health, relationship with his wife and children, happiness?

The Case of Joseph M.

Joseph is a boy of 14. His parents are poor, and they live in a tenement house in New York. In order to help out at home, Joseph has a job after school, and on Saturdays and Sundays. Although his clothes are old, he keeps them neatly pressed. Joseph wants to become a doctor, and he started a savings account to put money away for his college education. His grades in school are excellent. Whenever he is given a job to do, he does it promptly and carefully. His fellow students look up to him and respect his leadership. Somehow he finds time for the Boy Scouts, and he has earned enough merit badges to become an Eagle Scout. Joseph is a club leader at the settlement house and has been a fine influence on the younger boys.

What is your prediction about Joseph's future?

The Case of Margaret L.

Margaret is in her second year of high school. She is extremely popular and has dates three or four times during the week. Her grades are poor. Margaret spends a great deal of time on the telephone. Her mother no longer begs her to study. She sneers at her father because he doesn't earn enough money to buy her all the pretty dresses she wants. Margaret was supposed to have the leading role in the class play, but she didn't learn her lines and the dramatics coach replaced her. Margaret then said that the play wasn't any good. She took piano lessons for a while, but stopped because she didn't want to practice. She borrows things from her girl friends, but seldom returns them. If she feels she must, she tells lies. She meets her boy friends at the corner drugstore but tells her parents that she was studying with a friend. Money disappears from the house, but Margaret insists that she didn't take it. Shortly after some money was missed, Margaret came home with a new bracelet. She said her aunt had given it to her. The aunt denied this, but Margaret burst into tears when the subject was mentioned, so the family decided to forget the whole thing.

What is your prediction about Margaret's future?

Without Magic

"I think you will agree that we know enough about these three people to predict their futures. We cannot be certain, of course. But we don't need a crystal ball or tea leaves to prophesy trouble for Mr. R. and Margaret L. And it is reasonable to assume that Joseph M. will be the same kind of responsible man that he is a boy, and that he will realize his ambition of becoming a doctor. There is no magic in these predictions. We don't have to be fortune-tellers to guess at these futures."

Rabbi Mayer walked to the blackboard. "Here is one example of a profession that predicts the future." And he wrote:

A doctor predicts the future health of a patient by testing his temperature, the condition of his heart, blood pressure, blood count, pulse rate, etc.

"Can you think of other such professions?" asked the Rabbi.

Breaking the Law

"The Prophets were often able to predict the future by observation, through what they saw and heard. This they knew: those who broke God's laws and refused to obey His commandments would be punished. They believed in Ethical Monotheism. They knew that God hated injustice, corruption, and cruelty, and that the guilty could have no real happiness in the future. There are penalties for breaking the moral laws of God, just as there are penalties for breaking other laws."

Gary asked to speak. "I've never thought of it that way, Rabbi. I can see that if someone disobeys the law, he will be punished. But suppose he isn't caught and gets away with it?"

"He will never get away with it," insisted Helaine. "Sooner or later he will be caught. But even if he isn't, he's hurting himself, his own character."

"Let's look at it this way," said Rabbi Mayer. "A man may go through a red light and get away with it. But if he does it again and again, the chances are that he will be caught. There is something more important, however. This man is endangering his own life and the life of others. I remember a man who came into my study and cried as he told me how he had disobeyed the traffic laws, and had run over a child. He was punished by the law, but a much greater punishment was in store for him. He suffered every time he remembered how he had held the lifeless body of that child in his arms. He suffered every time he thought of the grief of that child's mother.

"You wouldn't expect to jump from a tall building, defy the law of gravity, and not get hurt, would you? Whoever breaks the laws of nature will be punished in some way. The same thing is true of the moral laws of God. The Prophets knew that those who broke the moral laws of God would suffer the punishment of unhappiness.

The Bribe

"Sometimes people break the law and then try to bribe their way out. People may give gifts to others for selfish purposes. In ancient times, people tried to bribe a God of magic with gifts—gifts that were called sacrifices. They believe that God liked these sacrifices, and that He would protect them from their enemies and forgive their sins if they gave Him burnt offerings of animals.

"The Prophets scoffed at these bribes. They insisted that God wanted justice and righteousness rather than sacrifice, and that the people did not please God with their offerings.

"It took great courage for Amos, the fearless Prophet of Tekoa, to go into enemy country at Beth-El. The people had gathered there for a feast, and the High Priest was preparing a sacrifice, but Amos declared in the name of God:

> *I hate, I despise your feasts,*
> *And I will take no delight in your solemn assemblies.*
> *Yea, though ye offer me burnt-offerings and your meal*
> *offerings,*
> *I will not accept them;*
> *Neither will I regard the peace-offerings of your fat beasts.*
> *Amos 5:21–22*

"How it startled the people to hear the words of this courageous man of God! God hated their feasts, and their offerings were not acceptable. But what did God want? Amos told them:

> *Let justice well up as the waters,*
> *And righteousness as a mighty stream.*

"This was the commandment of the Still, Small Voice. This is what God wanted: JUSTICE! RIGHTEOUSNESS! Religion was a way of life, a life of just and righteous deeds.

"Amos predicted disaster because the people were not obeying the moral laws of God. He was not a foreteller using magic or superstition. He was a forthteller who proclaimed the requirements of a God of Justice: justice from those who worshipped Him.

"The prophet Isaiah predicted the future too. He predicted destruction and misery. God would punish those who broke His laws. He too, spoke against sacrifices instead of justice, as he proclaimed in the name of God:

> *To what purpose is the multitude of your sacrifices unto Me?*
> *Saith the Lord;*
> *I am full of the burnt-offerings of rams,*
>   *And the fat of fed beasts;*
> *And I delight not in the blood*
> *Of bullocks, or of lambs, or of he-goats. . . .*
> *Wash you, make you clean,*
> *Put away the evil of your doings from before Mine eyes.*
> *Cease to do evil; learn to do well;*
> *Seek justice, relieve the oppressed,*
> *Judge the fatherless, plead for the widow.*
>
>   *Isaiah 1:11–17*

"Isaiah didn't care about being popular. He didn't care what the people thought or said. There was something more important than being liked. He had to speak because his God demanded it. He had to warn the people of the consequences of their actions:

> *Woe unto them that join house to house,*
> *Who add field to field,*
> *Until there is no space left,*
> *And they dwell alone in the midst of the land.*
>
> *Woe unto them that rise at dawn*
> *To pursue strong drink,*
> *Who tarry late into the night*
> *Until wine inflames them . . .*

But they regard not the work of the Lord
And see not what His hands have made . . .

Woe unto them that call evil good, and good evil . . .
Woe unto them that are wise in their own eyes . . .
Therefore, as the fire devours stubble
And as hay shrivels in a flame,
So their root shall be as rottenness
And their blossom go up as dust;
Because they have rejected the teaching of the Lord of hosts,
And despised the word of the Holy One of Israel.

Isaiah 5:8 ff.

Rabbi Mayer paused. The class seemed to be listening still to the eloquence of Isaiah's warning. "I've talked for quite a while," said the Rabbi. "Now I'm going to give you a chance to explain how we can apply the words of the prophets to our own time."

AMOS AT TIMES SQUARE

1 Rabbi Jacob Weinstein of Chicago once wrote his impressions of what the prophet Amos would have said if he appeared at Times Square in New York. Suppose Amos did walk down the streets of New York today? What would he say about our civilization? Would he find fault with our treatment of the poor and oppressed? What would he think of the way we worship God? Would he approve of the way we practice our religious faith? Could he apply what he said in Chapter 5, Verse 21, to our temples and synagogues today? What might Amos say to us today? Complete the following lines, using the language and the observance of our times.

I hate, I despise your _____
And I will take no delight in your _____
Yea, though ye offer me _____
I will not accept them;

> *Neither will I regard the* _____
> *Take away from Me the noise of thy* _____
> *And let Me not hear the* _____
> *But let justice well up as the waters,*
> *And righteousness as a mighty stream.*

2 How would the following react to Amos' statements?
  The Rabbi of the Temple
  The President and Board of Trustees of the Temple
  The local press
  The Anti-Defamation League of B'nai B'rith
  The House UnAmerican Activities Committee
  The American Civil Liberties Union

3 Would Amos be asked to speak at a national Jewish convention? Before Congress? Would he be invited to fashionable homes as a guest at dinner parties?

  What would Amos say about:
  Freedom of speech
  Soviet Russia
  Race relations
  Corruption in government
  The American Indians
  Labor-Management problems, strikes, and wages

4 There are nine chapters in the Book of Amos. Read them carefully, and make a list of the corrupt practices that also apply to our own society.

5 How would you apply the statement of Isaiah, at the top of page 82, to modern times?

Isaiah Before the United Nations

Everything seemed so strange to him. Not long ago, he had been comfortable and secure in the home of his father Amoz. King Uzziah had liked him and he was a favorite at the court. But Uzziah had died, and he had prayed that the new king, Jotham, would bring justice to the oppressed. Suddenly Jotham died, and there was a new king on the throne. Ahaz was a coward, and his heart trembled as a tree of the forest trembles with the wind. He had warned Ahaz, and then he remembered the terrible destruction and the misery that visited his native land.

But how did he get to twentieth-century America, with its tall buildings, honking horns, swift monsters of the sky, and strange talk—that was the most confusing of all. Slowly he began to remember. God had decided to send a prophet to the United Nations to beg for peace. Isaiah could hear again the voice of God, saying:

> *Whom shall I send,*
> *And who will go for us?*

And he had answered:

> *Here am I!*
> *Send me!*

Now he stood before the cool glass skyscraper overlooking the river, trying to summon the courage to enter. Men and women called "delegates" spoke many languages as they rushed past him. Perhaps he shouldn't have come here. But he had volunteered to speak to the United Nations in behalf of God. He had been sent on a mission, and he must not fail his God. How could he make the nations of the world understand, when he knew only one language? And then his heart leaped with joy as he heard two men converse in a vaguely familiar tongue. Their speech was odd, but he could understand them! Yes, he could understand. They spoke about war—but a war without spears, bows and arrows, or battering rams. It was strange talk about atom bombs and hydrogen bombs. He did not understand them, but he knew they must be terrible beyond all words. These men feared total destruction, and he was reminded of the warning of God, when in his own time

and in his own land he once asked: *"Lord! How long?"* And God
answered him:

> *Until the cities are in ruin without an inhabitant,*
> *And the houses without a human occupant,*
> *And the land become utterly desolate.*

No! This must not happen again. Isaiah would speak to these
men. And they were amazed to hear him speak in the very same
Hebrew that they had used to study the Bible. Afterwards they told
him they were delegates from the new State of Israel, and that they
spoke modern Hebrew. Now Isaiah knew why their language
sounded so strange and yet so familiar. Joy filled his being and
reverence gripped his heart as he realized that God had preserved

his people throughout the long centuries, and that Israel was a member of the United Nations. But enough of these thoughts. He had a mission to perform. He must speak to the entire group of delegates in the name of God. His new friends promised to help, and to translate his remarks for the interpreters.

Soon Isaiah was escorted into the hall. A buzz of excitement swept through the assembly. Who was this strange man? What nation did he represent? Who gave him the right to speak? The chairman rapped for order. The General Assembly of the United Nations was now in session. Isaiah was recognized, and he took his place before the microphones. He looked out at a sea of eager faces. Men and women with strange contraptions around their heads—earphones—waited to hear his words.

His voice was calm as he began: "You ask who I am. My name is Isaiah, and I come to you out of the past. You ask what nation I represent. I represent humanity. I echo the voice of humanity, crying for peace. Who gave me the right to speak? The King of all Kings, the Holy One, Blessed be His Name, has commanded me to speak. Thus saith the Lord God."

The delegates listened in wonder to this strange appeal for justice, international understanding, and world peace. They trembled when Isaiah predicted destruction if they ignored the moral commandments of God. The hall echoed with the power of his voice:

> *Keep ye justice and do righteousness . . Seek ye the Lord while He may be found. Call ye upon Him while He is near. Let the wicked forsake his ways, and let the man of iniquity his thoughts: and let him return unto the Lord and He will have compassion upon him.*

God was appealing to them to repent and change their ways. The future would bring happiness and peace to all—if the nations would hear the voice of God. The Still, Small Voice would lead nations

to a society of the kingdom of God, and the fulfillment of the hopes
and dreams of the religious teachers of all ages. Isaiah concluded:

It shall come to pass, in the end of days,
That the mountain of the Lord's house shall be established
at the top of the mountains,
And shall be exalted above the hills;
And all nations shall flow unto it.
And many peoples shall go and say,
Come ye, and let us go up to the mountain of the Lord,
To the house of the God of Jacob;
And He will teach us of His ways,
And we will walk in His paths.
For out of Zion shall go forth the law,
And the word of the Lord from Jerusalem,
And He shall judge between the nations,
And arbitrate for many peoples;
And they shall beat their swords into ploughshares
And their spears into pruning hooks;
Nation shall not lift up sword against nation,
Neither shall they learn war any more.

Isaiah said a silent prayer. He descended from the rostrum,
walked down the aisle, and left the United Nations as he returned
to the past and took his place in the archives of history.

Prophets of Today

Gary sighed. "Oh, if we only had prophets today! If we only had
an Amos at Times Square, or an Isaiah at the United Nations."

"We do have prophets today," said Rabbi Mayer. "But we don't
always recognize them as prophets. Nor do we always respect them
for their courageous actions or their fearless speech. There are devoted men and women in every generation who speak to us in the

name of God. But we refuse to listen to them, and sometimes we even persecute them for their thoughts and actions."

"Are there any modern Jewish prophets?" asked Henry.

"There are prophets among all peoples and all faiths, Henry," said the Rabbi. "However, I will tell you about three rabbis and a layman who lived up to the noblest traditions of social justice established by the ancient prophets of Israel."

Courage in New Orleans

Dr. Ralph Bunche, a prominent Negro attorney, served as a mediator in the dispute between the Jews and the Arabs, when the United Nations created the State of Israel as a democratic commonwealth. A civic group in New Orleans invited him to speak to them. Dr. Bunche accepted the invitation on the condition that there be no segregation of white or colored people at this meeting. The community of New Orleans was not accustomed to having Negroes and Whites sit together at the same meeting, and the committee tried desperately to find an auditorium where a non-segregated meeting might be held. But no hall could be found.

Rabbi Julian Feibelman of Temple Sinai had the courage to go to his Board of Trustees for permission to use the large and beautiful Temple for that meeting. When the congregation heard of this, some members became frightened and said: "No, there will be trouble. Why should we do this? Let others take the first step and we will follow." Some members threatened to resign. But Rabbi Feibelman pressed his case before the Board and reminded it of the prophetic heritage of Judaism. Inspired by their rabbi, they consented. The meeting was held in Temple Sinai. A large crowd filled the Temple. Jews and Christians, Negroes and Whites, met together and listened to a superb address by Dr. Bunche. There were no incidents. There was no trouble. After the meeting, the people of New Orleans, the press, and civic leaders praised Rabbi Feibelman and the congregation of Temple Sinai for having had the courage to live up to their principles. Later, Dr. Bunche was awarded the Nobel Prize for his contributions to the cause of peace. Rabbi Feibelman never received a prize for his fearless action, but he earned the deep respect and admiration of his fellow citizens.

Marked for Death

In 1933, when it seemed certain that the Nazis would rule Germany, its leading rabbi, Leo Baeck, was urged to flee to America. He refused to leave his people at a time of crisis, and continued to preach the word of God. The Nazis were furious with this man who, despite threats of punishment, continued to defy the Hitler terror. There was something about him that made them afraid. Without thought of his own safety, he served his people wherever they needed him.

Jews throughout the world wanted to do something to save this courageous man. In 1939, he was asked to become the rabbi of a congregation in Cincinnati, Ohio. Again and again he was urged to find safety and security in America. But Rabbi Baeck refused to leave Germany. He continued to preach about the eventual triumph of justice and the defeat of the Nazis. Finally, the Nazis put him in a concentration camp. But even there he would not be silenced. The lone, gaunt figure of the venerable rabbi was still seen helping his fellow Jews, even in the concentration camp of Theresienstadt. Many times the Nazis placed his name on the death list. But something always happened to save him. He was defying the Nazis and helping his people at the very time that the Nazis were forced to abandon the camps and scurry for safety before the liberating forces of the American and British armies. When the tiny remnant of the Jews of Germany was finally saved, the old and weary Rabbi Baeck consented to come to America, and train a new generation of rabbis. Many wonderful stories are told about this prophet of modern times, a man who was marked for death but who never lost his hope and faith in God.

The Prophet of Kansas City

On May 21, 1932, Rabbi Samuel Mayerberg of Temple B'nai Jehuda spoke to the Government Study Club of Kansas City on the subject of "A Non-Partisan and Non-Political Administration for Kansas City." He dared expose the corrupt political system that had plagued the people of Kansas City for many years. Rabbi Mayerberg attacked the political machine that brought evil, gangsterism, bribery, and injustice to his city. The city officials were angry. The gangsters raged and threatened. But nothing could induce Rabbi Mayerberg to be silent. Aided by other good citizens, he continued his fight for good government in Kansas City. Day after day, he exposed the corruption of the mayor, the police chief and the City Council. He revealed how the ballot boxes were stuffed with fraudulent votes. He showed how the political bosses worked hand in hand with gangsters. The gangsters tried to bribe him. Threats were made against his life. Prominent members of the congregation came to him and told him to stop his efforts to rid Kansas City of corrupt government. Some members of his Temple resigned. Pressure was brought to bear on his Board of Trustees. Businessmen in his congregation found that their stores were boycotted, and sometimes closed down. When the Rabbi conducted religious services, a bodyguard was with him. He slept with a revolver near his bed. Friends told him, "Forget it, Rabbi. What can you do? You are only ruining your health and your life!" Rabbi Mayerberg did not listen. He continued his fight for honesty and decency until the corrupt government was defeated, and the good people of Kansas City began to restore decency, justice and courage to their community. Today, Rabbi Mayerberg is respected and honored for his prophetic courage, and for the great service he rendered to the people of Kansas City.

The People's Attorney

Not all modern prophets are rabbis. Louis Dembitz Brandeis was not a rabbi, but he devoted his life to the cause of social justice. As a brilliant young lawyer, he took cases that seemed hopeless to others, for he believed there is always hope for a just cause. And he won many of these seemingly hopeless cases for the downtrodden and helpless.

When President Woodrow Wilson nominated Brandeis to the Supreme Court of the United States in 1916, there were many who opposed him. They called him "radical," and "troublemaker," but the nomination was confirmed. On June 5, 1916, Brandeis donned the robes of an Associate Justice. For more than twenty-two years he served the cause of truth and righteousness in America.

Louis Brandeis hated tyranny and corruption in any form. Independent of spirit, he did not hesitate to disagree with the majority if he thought it wrong. His enemies sneered at him and called him "the people's attorney" and "the friend of the little man," but Brandeis regarded these as compliments. It did not matter whether a man was rich or poor, powerful or weak. His decisions were influenced only by his convictions and his love of truth.

This great Supreme Court Justice was criticized and condemned because of his court decisions. He was often ridiculed for his devotion to the Zionist cause. He was the target of attacks by those who thought he took too active a part in the effort to achieve peace. But Brandeis shrugged off the criticisms and the attacks. He was too busy making his contribution to a better world, a world of truth, justice, and peace.

Giants of the Spirit

"And we always thought the prophets were some kind of fortunetellers!" said Jonathan. "It takes a lot of courage to be a prophet."

"It takes more than courage, Jonathan." Rabbi Mayer closed his notebook. "It takes a great sensitivity to hear the Still, Small Voice, and to obey that voice no matter how great the opposition may be. The prophets were spokesmen of God. They condemned evil, pleaded for justice, and appealed to the people to live by the commandments of the Jewish faith. Sometimes they were tortured. Sometimes they were imprisoned. All too often they were hated, ridiculed and despised. But with a magnificent stubbornness, they persisted. They cleaved to the truth, and proclaimed that a God of Justice demanded justice from those who worshipped Him. The prophets of yesterday and today have been called "Giants of the Spirit." They towered above all other men; their teachings are our precious heritage of prophetic Judaism. I hope we may be worthy of that heritage."

QUESTIONS FOR DISCUSSION

1 How can we apply prophetic Judaism to our own lives? Which of our problems call for prophetic action? In what ways can we be spokesmen for God?

2 In what way does the sermon of Isaiah (58:1–9) apply to Jewish life today?

3 How can we tell the difference between a false prophet and a true prophet? Explain the significance of Deuteronomy 18:13–22; I Kings 22:1–37.

4 What do the stories of Naboth's vineyard (I Kings 21), and Nathan and David (II Samuel 11:1–12:15), teach us about prophetic Judaism?

5 What did Amos try to teach by his statement: "Are ye not as the children of the Ethiopians unto Me, O children of Israel? saith the Lord" (Amos 9:7)? How can we apply this in our relationships with other peoples?

6 The prophet Malachi asked: "Have we not all one Father? Hath not one God created us? Why do we deal treacherously every man against his brother, profaning the covenant of our fathers?" What did he mean? In what way are these vital questions today?

7 What does Micah 6:6–8 teach us about what God demands of us today? Do you agree or disagree with Micah? Why?

8 The prophet Habakkuk said: "The righteous shall live by his faith" (Habakkuk 2:4). How can someone your age actually live by his faith?

9 In what ways is Christianity indebted to the prophets of Israel?

10 Why do you think the Jews were the first to develop prophets of social justice?

11 What do you think Justice Louis Brandeis meant when he said: "The twentieth century ideals of America have been the ideals of the Jew for twenty centuries"?

SELECTED QUOTATIONS

Fearless and Undaunted

The company of inspired men, commonly known as the prophets of Israel, were the unique product of the Jewish religious genius. They were preeminently preachers of righteousness. Fearless and undaunted, they told the house of Israel their sins and the house of Jacob their transgressions. They contemplated the facts of life from the highest point of view. For them religion and morality were blended, ethics and politics were one. Theirs was peculiarly a social message; the demand for justice underlies all their thinking and speaking. They had a veritable passion for righteousness; through all the ages their words have been torches lighting the way of men struggling upward toward the truth.

RABBI DAVID PHILIPSON

Perfect Ideal of Religion

In the eighth century B.C., in the heart of a world of idolatrous poly-theists, the Hebrew prophets put forth a conception of religion which appears to me to be as wonderful an inspiration of genius as the art of Phidias or the science of Aristotle.

"And what doth the Lord require of thee, but to do justly, and to love mercy, and to walk humbly with thy God?"

If any so-called religion takes away from this great saying of Micah, I think it wantonly mutilates, while, if it adds thereto, I think it obscures the perfect ideal of religion.

THOMAS HUXLEY

The Courage of the Prophets

The way of prophecy is not always easy. The prophets of old were not always greeted by applause, nor were they popular idols. They were compelled frequently to say harsh things, but true, about their friends, about their society, about conditions and their own community. Those in positions of power and privilege at times resented their message, became indignant at their challenge, and persecuted, exiled and outlawed them.

RABBI FERDINAND M. ISSERMAN
This Is Judaism

A Rabbi Fights a Political Machine

Constant threat came from the underworld; my campaign was hurting their illegal gains, and if we succeeded in recalling the Council and procuring a faithful City Manager, their rackets would be entirely eliminated. As I drove to a North Side meeting one night, my car was forced to the curb and a shot was fired. Fortunately, friends had equipped my car with bullet-proof glass. After this incident the Governor, upon the insistence of friends, assigned to me two men, deputized as deputy coroners. The idea of having armed guards accompany me everywhere I went was extremely distasteful. They not only drove the car, but also placed me between them when I walked through overflow crowds to meeting places. They even guarded homes (against my wish) in which I officiated at weddings and funerals. They attended all Temple services. When I protested, they said simply, "We are under orders." During this time, while I realized my life was in constant jeopardy through attack of some dope fiend or sly gangster, I experienced no real personal fear, though, I confess, I had the constant dread that my precious wife, just convalescing from an operation that nearly took her life, might in some way be harmed. Thugs and kidnappers under the protection of Lazia and his more respectable political friends found a safe haven in Kansas City. Ransoms were often collected there. For months, though I refused to be armed at any time, I never went to sleep at night without a loaded pistol on the floor beside my bed.

RABBI SAMUEL MAYERBERG,
Chronicle Of An American Crusader

Courage in the Shadow of Fear

In Jewry's darkest hour, Dr. Baeck also kept the intellectual and religious flame alive. To be caught imparting knowledge meant death, but Baeck determined to do something for the morale of the camp. He let it be known that he would lecture at certain barracks. Under cover of complete darkness and unsuspected by the Storm Troopers, hundreds huddled together to hear the Rabbi lecture on Plato, Aristotle, Spinoza and Kant. Week after week, without notes or books of any kind, this man, out of the granary of his mind, fed his hungry people.

RABBI JOSHUA LOTH LIEBMAN

The Shame of Our City

Certainly the cumulative evidence of corruption and gangsterism in high places and low would give ample texts for some modern-day Amos who strayed from his sheep and found himself caught in the revolving door of our City Hall. One can imagine him standing there on Randolph and Clark thundering this litany:

For ye murder in cold blood those who would speak even a lesser lie in the streets;

Your meat inspectors take rich bribes that they may not note the difference between a horse and a cow;

Your guardians of the law permit men of violence to bar the children of Ethiopia from their rightful homes;

They encourage triggerhappy Shamisim to rain death upon the innocent.

Your judges bend the pregnant hinges of the knee, knowing that gangster favors follow such fawning;

They give probation to reckless destroyers in the teeth of all reason and snarl cynically, "Sue me."

Your public servants are like those shameful sons of Eli who take the juicy meat with a 3-pronged fork from the public pot and leave the watered soup to the hungry people. . . ."

RABBI JACOB J. WEINSTEIN

THINGS TO DO

1 Debate the proposition: RESOLVED: That rabbis advance the cause of Prophetic Judaism by their participation in politics.

2 Write an essay on the modern significance of Isaiah's statement, "My House shall be called a House of Prayer for all peoples."

3 Arrange discussion groups with one topic assigned to each group:
  a Rabbis should take action to eliminate Bible readings from the public schools.
  b The problem of Christmas in the public schools:
      Should Jewish children sing Christmas carols?
      Is it proper for Jewish children to participate in Christmas plays?
      Should we favor joint Hanukkah-Christmas programs in the public schools?
  c Should Jews take action in controversial affairs of the community?
  d What should Jews do to promote better relations between the white and colored races?

e The answer of the Prophets to Fascism and Communism.

f If the Prophets were with us today.

g What the Prophets mean to Orthodox, Conservative and Reform Judaism today.

4 Look up the following verses and then describe what each Prophet endured in order to obey the Still, Small Voice:

I Kings 18:4; I Kings 22:27; Amos 7:12–13;

Jeremiah 20:2; 32:2; 37:15; 38:6.

5 Choose a class project for the year—a concrete program to further a specific cause of social justice.

6 Prepare the dramatic choral reading "The Prophets Speak" (Union of American Hebrew Congregations) as an assembly program.

7 Look up I Kings 18:17–18, and compare Justice Brandeis with Elijah.

8 What injustices would you protest if you were a prophet? What action would you propose to correct these injustices?

SUGGESTED READINGS

Cronbach, Abraham, *The Bible and Our Social Outlook*, Chapter V.

Gamoran, Mamie, *The Voice of the Prophets*, Bible Reader V.

Isserman, Ferdinand M., *This Is Judaism*, pp. 32–63.

Landman, Isaac, *Stories of the Prophets*.

Levine, Raphael, *The Legacy of the Prophets*, a pamphlet.

Mayerberg, Samuel, *Chronicle of an American Crusader*, Chapter IV.

Steinbach, Alexander A., *What Is Judaism*, pp. 7–11.

The Universal Jewish Encyclopedia, Prophets and Prophecy, Vol. 8, pp. 658–664.

6

THE VOICE OF THE PSALMIST

The Holiness of Man

The Robot of Clay

"In the year 1580, on the second day of the month of March, just as the clock struck midnight, Judah Lowe of Prague proceeded with his plan to create a Golem, a robot-man of clay.

"Accompanied by two friends, he went to the outskirts of the city, to the banks of the Moldau River, and found a bed of clay. Then he began to fashion the clay into the figure of a man. Working with desperate haste, chanting from the *Sefer Yetzirah*, the Book of Mystery, he formed the Golem out of clay, and the robot lay before him with its face turned toward heaven.

"Now Judah walked slowly around the clay body, from right to left. He looked, and behold! the body became red as fire. With growing terror in his heart, he saw the fire-redness fade from the body as water flowed through it. Hair grew on its head, and nails on its fingers and toes. But the Golem was not alive!

"The sages walked around the figure once again, and placed in its mouth a parchment with the name of God written on it. Bowing to the east and the west, the south and the north, all three recited together:

> *And he breathed into his nostrils the breath of life*
> *And man became a living soul!*

"They looked again, and the Golem opened its eyes. They said to it: 'Stand up!' and it stood up.

"Three men had assembled at midnight to create a robot-man, a Golem. At daybreak, four men walked homeward."

Eldon put down the mimeographed page. "That's a strange tale," he thought. "I wonder why the Rabbi asked us to read it as our assignment for the 'Ethics of the Psalms.' Such a creepy story! Imagine a robot-man made out of clay! The Rabbi told us it was just a legend, that it never really happened, but. . . ."

Getting up from his chair, Eldon stretched, and then walked into the kitchen for a cold drink. He took a bottle opener from the drawer, flipped off the cap, and with the bottle of soda in his hand, he returned to his chair and settled himself. "Maybe the rest of the assignment will help me figure out what this is all about." And he picked up the second page and began to read.

The Machine That Acted Human

"The site of the legendary creation of the Golem was in Prague. The time: the sixteenth century. Almost four hundred years later, in the city of Cambridge, Massachusetts, scientists at Harvard

University created a modern golem, a robot, a machine so closely resembling a human being that it was given a name: Mark III. This robot was called 'the human brain.' It could calculate figures into the billions in a fraction of a second. Mark III could walk, talk, answer questions, and even work out the most complicated mathematical problems. But Mark III was not a human being. It behaved like one, but something was missing. What did Mark III lack that made it a machine and not a man?"

The doorbell rang. Eldon got up and went to the door and there was his friend, Lee. "Hi, Eldon. I've read these assignments three or four times and I can't figure them out. Do you know what all of this means, and what it has to do with the Psalms?"

"I don't understand it any more than you do, Lee," said Eldon. "But I haven't finished my reading. Here's something called 'Questions and Clues.' Let's try and work it out together."

QUESTIONS

1　Was the Golem of Judah Lowe really a man? Give the reasons for your answer.

2　What is the difference between a beast and a human being?

3　Why wasn't Mark III a human being?

4　What was it that Mark III lacked that made it a machine and n a man?

5　What kind of decisions and choices was Mark III unable to make?

CLUES

1　Open your Bible and read Genesis 1:27 and 11:7.

2　Read Deuteronomy 30:15–16; 19–20; Psalm 8:5–6.

The Chemistry Chart

When the class assembled the next day, all attention was directed to the blackboard. This is what the class saw:

Oxygen	65%	Calcium	1.5%	Sodium	.15%
Carbon	18%	Phosphorus	1.0%	Chlorine	.05%
Hydrogen	10%	Potassium	.35%	Magnesium	.05%
Nitrogen	3%	Sulphur	.25%	Iron	.004%
		Iodine	.00004%		

"What is this," asked Mildred, "a lesson in chemistry or a lesson on the ethics of the Psalms?"

Everyone had his own theory, but no one was quite sure. Rabbi Mayer entered the room and went directly to the blackboard. Pointing to the chart, he said: "I assume you were trying to guess the meaning of this chart. It is a chart of the chemical elements that make up the human body. If we were to estimate the worth of a human being in terms of these chemical elements, the amount would be about $1.25. But I'm sure you will agree that a person is worth much more. A human being is more than flesh and bone and sinew. Man is more than clay, more than a combination of atoms and molecules. That's why I asked you to read the stories of the Golem of Prague and the modern scientific wonder called Mark III.

"According to the legend, the Golem could walk. It obeyed commands. It looked like a man. It acted like a man. But the Golem was not a man. It did not have a will of its own. It could not determine the difference between right and wrong, good and evil.

"And Mark III? Mark lacked a soul. Mark was not created in the image of God, but in the image of a blueprint, in the likeness of a machine.

"Now we must ask ourselves: How does Judaism look upon man? As a child of God, created in the image of God, a sacred personality endowed with a soul? Or as a golem of clay, a robot of steel, a combination of chemical elements, will-less and soul-less?

What Is Man?

"The ancient Hebrew Psalmist asked that same question. He looked at the heavens and experienced an overwhelming sense of awe before the wonders of God's creation, and he exclaimed:

> *When I behold Thy heavens, the work of Thy fingers, the moon and the stars which Thou hast established; What is man that Thou art mindful of him? and the son of man that Thou thinkest of him? Yet, Thou hast made him but little lower than the angels, and hast crowned him with glory and honor.*   *Psalm 8:4–6*

"The Psalmist knew that his answer to the question, 'What is man?' would determine his attitude toward God, toward the world in which he lived, and even toward himself. And his answer was that man is but little lower than the angels. This doesn't mean that we believe in angels. It means that man is holy, sacred, and precious to God, and that man should be sacred and precious to his fellow man.

"Do you understand what the Psalmist meant? He was trying to tell us that man is more than clay or chemistry. Man is created in the image of God. All men are children of God. And each of us has the responsibility to help the other.

The Voice of God

"If we listened closely, perhaps we would hear the voice of God speaking to us, asking us what we are going to do about the hungry, the weak. What are we going to do about the troubled, we who are more fortunate? What are we going to do about the oppressed and enslaved everywhere, the people who yearn for freedom, who live out their years in the shadow of fear? Are they not all created in the image of God? Are they not all but little lower than the angels?

"Do the words of the Psalmist seem clearer now? Because man is a child of God, created in the image of God, man must become worthy of being a part of God. The Psalmist teaches us to be responsible for all men, to devote ourselves to helping all people, regardless of their color or their religion. They are all our brothers, because we are all children of God."

The Image of God

Rabbi Mayer paused. "Every time I talk about the Psalms, every time I read the Psalms, I find new inspiration in their magnificent teachings. It is not easy to grasp their meaning. We have to think about them, ponder over them, learn to appreciate their holiness and their wisdom.

"I know I've talked for a long time, and I know you must have many questions. But we cannot understand Judaism as a way of life, we cannot solve the mystery of the Still, Small Voice, until we answer the question, 'what is man?', until we see that man is but little lower than the angels, that he is created in the image of God."

Jerry raised his hand, and when the Rabbi called on him, he said: "I don't quite understand what you mean by the image of God. You don't mean that man looks like God, or that God looks like man, do you?"

"That's a good question, Jerry," replied Rabbi Mayer, "about a very difficult concept. You are right when you say that man is not created in the physical image of God. Man is created in the spiritual image of God."

The God Within Us

The Rabbi could see that Jerry was still perplexed. "Let's put it this way, Jerry," he continued. "Everyone has a soul. We can't explain exactly what a soul is. No one has ever seen a soul. We can't analyze it or dissect it in a laboratory. The soul is a part of God within us. It's like a receiving set. It listens to God, and it speaks to God. The body dies, but the soul lives forever. The soul can never die. It is a part of God."

Lucille asked, "But when we say that man has a soul and is created in the image of God, does it mean that man has a part of God in him all the time?"

"That's right, Lucille. When we speak of the image of God within man, we mean that man has the capacity for truth, for holiness, for beauty, for goodness. We mean that there is a part of God within man; we mean that man is holy. By doing deeds of kindness, unselfishness, and helpfulness, through the godly qualities of mercy, truth and justice, we show that we are a part of God and that God is a part of us.

"This is a very complex idea," continued the Rabbi. "The image of God does not refer to a body, but to the soul, and to our capacity for mercy, truth, goodness and holiness. It is the God within us."

Eldon had a question. "Does this mean, Rabbi, that only the soul is good, and that the body is bad?"

I'm glad you asked that, Eldon," said Rabbi Mayer," because I don't want you to think that the body is bad, that Judaism regards the body as evil.

"In just a little while, I'm going to talk about how the Psalmist found God, even in the wonders of the human body. Judaism teaches that the body is the dwelling-place of the soul; therefore the body is holy. We respect the body and keep it clean and pure because it is the 'temple of the soul.' The rabbis tell a story about the body, and the importance of caring for it.

Hillel and his Pupils

"Hillel had finished the lesson with his pupils and was preparing to leave when they said to him: 'Master, where are you going?' 'To perform a religious duty,' he replied.

" 'Which religious duty?'

" 'To bathe in the bathhouse,' he answered.

"They asked: 'How is bathing a religious duty?' And Hillel said: 'If someone is paid to clean the statues of the king in the theatres and circuses, and furthermore associates with the nobility, how much more so should I, who am created in the divine image and likeness, take care of my body.' (Lev. R. 34:3)

"You see," continued Rabbi Mayer, "Hillel believed it a religious duty to keep his body clean, because he was created in the divine image.

"These are not easy concepts. We must think about them carefully to see how Judaism teaches that both the body and the soul are holy, and that man is but little lower than the angels. Perhaps we should stop right here and see how we can apply this teaching to our own lives, how the belief that man is created in the image of God should influence our actions and attitudes."

QUESTIONS FOR DISCUSSION

1 How should the knowledge that there is a part of God within you make you respect yourself even more? How can self-respect make you a better person? How can you bring honor or dishonor to the God within you?

2 How should the awareness of God within you influence you with regard to:

Personal hygiene and care of the body

Personal habits

Purity of thought and speech

Decency of character

3 How does the belief that man is created in the image of God bring you closer to God? Does it change your ideas of God in any way?

4 Read Genesis, Chapter 4:8–10. In what way do we sometimes give the answer of Cain?

5 How should the belief that there is a part of God within every human being influence our actions and attitudes toward others?

6 Can you show that you believe that man is "but little lower than the angels" in your relationships with your friends and classmates? How?

7 If we are all children of God, and responsible for our fellow men, what should we do in the following cases:

   a Children in your city live in a dirty, unsanitary neighborhood. Should you say: "I'm just a kid, what can I do?" What can you do about it?

   b You are asked to give some time after school to help with the Community Chest drive. This means giving up plans for sports or play. It means you will have to stay up a little later to do your homework. What should you do?

Wonderful Are Thy Works

Rabbi Mayer continued: "The Psalmist found God in the marvels of nature, in the order of the planets, and in the wonders of the human body. To him, God was the Master Engineer of the universe, the Supreme Architect of the world, and the Divine Sculptor who fashioned the human body. And the Psalmist said:

> *I will give thanks unto Thee, for I am fearfully and wonder-*
> *fully made;*
> *Wonderful are Thy works*
> *And that my soul knoweth right well.*

Psalm 139:14

"The Psalmist did not have the vast storehouse of modern science and medicine to draw upon. But through the Still, Small Voice, he learned how God is found in the wondrous construction of the human body. Thousands of years later, as scientists and physicians learned more about the physical nature of man, they too stood in awe before the talking, breathing, moving, thinking human being. They too felt humble before the wonder of life, and the miraculous growth of the child within its mother's body.

"Recently, a scientist, Dr. Edmund Brasset, said that he had found God through the human body, 'the most ingeniously contrived mechanism, the most beautiful structure on earth. Every bone is a masterpiece of architectural design. Every organ is a marvel of efficiency which no engineer can begin to equal. The smallest gland is a chemical plant that can outperform the greatest man-made laboratory in the world!' "

Rabbi Mayer paused. "Have you ever stopped to think of the wonders of the human body? We are told that the tissues of our bodies are composed of 28 billion cells. The blood delivers nourishment to each of the 28 billion cells, and the body does the rest, forming bone, nerves, and muscle . . . The human eye is a marvelous camera, receiving and sending picture images to the brain. The ear is a super-sensitive sound apparatus. The nervous system, with its millions of tiny nerve-endings, reaching every part of the body, carrying messages to the central station, the brain, is a master feat of engineering. We can understand why the Psalmist exclaimed:

I am fearfully and wonderfully made.

The Heavens Declare the Glory of God

Rabbi Mayer walked to the window and looked out for a moment. "The Still Small Voice spoke through the Psalmist, who beheld God not only in the wonderful construction of the human body, but also in the vastness and the order of God's universe.

"As he looked at the sun, the moon, and the stars, he felt himself in the presence of a mystery so awesome that he could only bow in reverence before the indescribable holiness of God.

"In recent times, Dr. Max T. Krohn experienced this sense of awe and mystery when he saw a photograph taken through the 200-inch telescope at Palomar—a picture of a star so far away that its light had taken billions or trillions of light years to reach that sensitized photographic plate, even though the light traveled at the speed of 186,324 miles a second. It is difficult for the human mind to comprehend such speed, or understand the vastness of time and space.

"You don't have to be an astronomer to get a sense of the vastness of the universe. Just learn the distance from New York to San Francisco. Then estimate how many times light could travel from New York to San Francisco and then back again in one second. If light travels 186,324 miles a second, how many miles would it travel in a minute? When you have the answer, figure out how many miles light would travel in an hour. Then go on to estimate how far light travels in a day, a month, a year.

"Dr. Krohn had seen a photograph of a star whose light had taken billions or trillions of light years to reach the photographic plate. This is the vastness that overwhelms us even today. How awesome it was to the Psalmist, who said:

> *The heavens declare the glory of God,*
> *And the firmament showeth His handiwork.*
>
> *Psalm 19:2*

God is Everywhere

"One of the most beautiful of all utterances," said Rabbi Mayer, "is to be found in Psalm 139, Verses 7-12:

> *Whither shall I go from Thy spirit?*
> *Or whither shall I flee from Thy presence?*
> *If I ascend up into heaven, Thou art there;*
> *If I make my bed in the netherworld, behold,*
>   *Thou art there.*

If I take the wings of the morning,
And dwell in the uttermost parts of the sea;
Even there would Thy hand lead me.
And Thy right hand would hold me.
And if I say: "Surely the darkness shall envelop me,
And the light about me shall be night";
Even the darkness is not too dark for Thee,
But the night shineth as the day;
The darkness is even as the light.

"The Psalmist knows that he never leaves the presence of God. Wherever he goes, God is there. The rabbis taught that God is not only in the heavens, but even in the humblest thornbush.

> An unbeliever asked a rabbi: "What purpose did your God have in speaking with Moses from the midst of a bush?" He answered: "To teach that there is no place without the Divine Presence, not even so lowly a thing as a bush." God said: "In every place where you find the imprint of men's feet, there am I." *Mechilta*

"Through the Still, Small Voice, the Psalmist realized that God sees every selfish and wrong act. God watches over him at all times; he must then always be clean of speech, pure of thought, and righteous in his deeds.

"The Psalmist is comforted by the knowledge of God's presence. When he is troubled, he can go to God and God will help him. When things go wrong and he is discouraged, God will give him new hope and confidence. He is never alone. Even though his friends may desert him, his God will never abandon him. With God's help, he will find the way to a new hope and a new tomorrow.

"The knowledge that God is everywhere helped the Psalmist. How can it help you?"

QUESTIONS FOR DISCUSSION

1   How can the belief that God is everywhere make you a better person? If you are tempted to do something wrong, will the knowledge that God is watching make you stop?

2   There are times when everything seems to go wrong. How can the belief that God is near help us?

3   Have you ever become ill at a time when you wanted to do something very badly, such as taking a trip, going to a party, or getting ready to leave for camp? Explain how faith in God can help a person get over the feeling of disappointment.

Fighting Our Fears

"The Psalms tell us how the Still, Small Voice can make us stronger, can help us fight our fears. There isn't a person in this world who hasn't been afraid of someone, or something, sometime," said Rabbi Mayer.

"Primitive man feared many things. He was afraid of the lightning and the rain. He was afraid of spirits, demons and ghosts. He knew so little; things he could not understand, or explain, he feared.

"Lewis Browne begins his book *This Believing World* with these words: 'In the beginning there was fear—and fear was in the heart of man, and fear controlled man.'

"Today, people are still afraid. Some fear sickness; some fear war. Some people are afraid of being a failure, or of being poor. Others are afraid of the dark, of walking under a ladder, or of breaking a mirror. At one time or another, everyone is afraid.

"We need help to overcome our fears. Fears are dangerous; they can do great harm.

"An Arab folk-story tells that Pestilence once met an Arab chief and informed him that it was on its way to Bagdad to take 5,000 lives. On its return from the city, Pestilence met the Arab again. 'You deceived me,' said the chief angrily. 'Instead of taking 5,000 lives, you took 50,000!'

"Pestilence replied: 'I, Pestilence, killed exactly 5,000. It was fear who killed the rest!'"

"The Psalmist found a way to conquer his fear. He listened to the Still, Small Voice. He discovered that his faith in God gave him strength to meet life's problems with courage. This is what he said:

> *The Lord is my light and my salvation;*
> *Whom shall I fear?*
> *The Lord is the stronghold of my life;*
> *Of whom shall I be afraid?*   *Psalm 27:1*

"This does not mean that the Psalmist was able to rid himself of all fears, but rather that his faith in God helped him control fear and made him strong.

"Do you think the hero never feels fear? Our military heroes tell us that they were afraid, in battle. But they did what they had to do, despite their fears. This is what courage means.

"Judaism does not offer us any miraculous cures for fear. But it does give us faith in God, faith that helps us master our fears, faith that helps us meet the challenges of life.

"Thus wrote the author of the 46th Psalm:

> *God is our refuge and strength,*
> *A very present help in trouble.*
> *Therefore will we not fear, though the earth do change,*
> *And though the mountains be moved into the heart of the*
> * seas;*
> *Though the waters thereof roar and foam,*
> *Though the mountains shake at the swelling thereof.*
>   *Psalm 46:2–4*

The Boy Who Was Always Afraid

"There is a story in Jewish literature of a boy who was always afraid. He was afraid of the dark. He was afraid of other boys. He was afraid to climb a tree or cross a stream of water. The slightest sound in the forest sent terror into his heart. At night he lay trembling in bed, the covers pulled over his head.

"One day his mother gave him a stout walking stick. She cut a notch in the stick, inserted a piece of paper with a single word written on it, and covered the notch with wood. The boy watched her with great curiosity, for he did not understand. Then his mother said: 'My son, I know you have many fears. Some day you will outgrow them. But I want you to be free and happy now. Here, take this stick. It contains a wonder-word, a word that will give you courage. Go now into the forest, and do not fear. The wonder-word will protect you.'

"The boy took the stick and walked into the forest. He heard the rustling of small animals, but he continued on. He saw a group of boys blocking his path, the very boys who had so often bullied and beaten him. But he did not run away. Holding his wonderful stick, he continued toward them. When the bullies saw their victim walking toward them, unafraid, they turned aside to let him pass.

"When the boy returned home after his walk in the forest, he ate his dinner and went to bed. That night he heard the sounds of the woods—the hooting of owls, the croaking of frogs, the rustling of leaves, even the noises of the house creaking in the silence of the night. But his stick was near him, and gave him courage. He slept soundly. No longer was he the boy who was always afraid.

"For the next few months he carried the stick with him wherever he went. When other boys attacked him, he fought back. Sometimes he won and sometimes he lost. He learned to climb trees with his friends. Often he was scratched and bruised but little things no longer frightened him.

"Now the boy began to think about the wonder-word in the stick. The more he thought about it, the more curious he became. At last he could wait no longer. And so he took a knife and removed the notch in the stick. His heart pounded as he lifted out the wonder-word. He looked and then he knew why his mother had called it a "wonder word." On the paper was written one word: GOD.

"Now he knew why the stick and the wonder-word had given him courage, why he had been able to do all the things that once had frightened him. It was because he had faith. He believed his wonder-word would help him. And because he had faith and believed in the power of the wonder-word, he had achieved courage, confidence, and strength.

"In the weeks and months that followed, the boy no longer carried the stick with him. Soon it was forgotten. But the wonder-word was never forgotten. He carried it with him wherever he went. The wonder-word was no longer in the stick; God was now in his heart!"

WHAT DO YOU THINK?

Read the following stories, and then tell how the Still, Small Voice can help us fight our fears.

Panic at the Pool

Marsha was afraid of the water. When she was eight years old, someone had pushed her off the edge of the pool into deep water. The lifeguard rescued her, but she was so terrified that she would never go near the water again.

As the years went by, Marsha wanted to learn how to swim. Knowing how much fun she was missing, she decided to register for lessons. As long as she was in shallow water, she wasn't too frightened. But when the instructor announced that after a ten minute rest, he would take each student into deeper water for individual instruction, Marsha became panicky. She rushed into the locker-room and began to cry. Her friend Sally tried to comfort her, but all Marsha could do was to sob over and over again: "I'm afraid! I'm afraid! I'm afraid!"

How could faith in God help Marsha fight her fear?

From Whence Shall Come My Help?

Larry was afraid of water, too. He took swimming lessons at the pool, and after a few lessons he was able to swim well enough to enjoy himself.

On Sunday afternoon, his friends, Milton and Philip, asked him to go out to the lake for a boat ride. The boat was old and rickety, but Larry was eager to go because now he knew how to swim.

After rowing in deep water for a while, Milton and Philip wanted to dive in for a swim. Larry was reluctant, but the boys urged him and he decided to jump in too.

He jumped! When he rose to the surface he began to kick his legs, but he couldn't manage to coordinate his body for swimming. He sank into the water, and came up again. Terrified, he started to scream, but the water choked him. Forgetting all the instructor had taught him, he struggled wildly in the water. He could hear his friends shouting: "We're coming. Just relax and float." But Larry continued to thrash about. He knew that if he could just relax, he would be all right. But fear had taken hold of him; he would drown before his friends reached him.

It was then that Larry thought of God. The words of the 121st Psalm flashed through his mind: "From whence shall my help come? My help cometh from the Lord Who made heaven and earth."

Larry became calm. He remembered the instructor's advice. He moved his legs in a bicycle kick, treading water. His friends reached him and helped him into the boat.

Did God really help Larry fight his fears?

QUESTIONS FOR DISCUSSION

1 Read Psalm 23. Explain why this psalm has been cherished by so many people in all generations.

2 What is meant by the words in Psalm 26:1:

Judge me, O Lord, for I have walked in my integrity.

What is integrity? How do you walk in your integrity?

3 What did the Psalmist mean when he said:

For Thou delightest not in sacrifice, else would I give it;
Thou hast no pleasure in burnt-offering.
The sacrifices of God are a broken spirit;
A broken and a contrite heart, O God, Thou wilt not despise.

Psalm 51:18–19

Why did God think a broken spirit and a contrite heart better than burnt-offerings?

4 Psalm 34:13 asks:

Who is the man that desireth life, and loveth days, that he may
see good therein?

Discuss in class the best way to achieve happiness in life. Then look up the answer of the Psalmist: Psalm 34:14. Why did the Psalmist give this answer? Do you agree with him?

5 Are the Psalms as acceptable to Christians as to Jews? Can Mo hammedans find inspiration and spiritual help in the Psalms?

6 What did the Psalmist mean when he said:

Create in me a clean heart, O God,
And renew a steadfast spirit within me. *Psalm 51:12*

How can Judaism help you obtain a clean heart and a steadfast spirit? What holy days are dedicated to this purpose?

7 Every one does things for which he is sorry and ashamed. The Psalmist was no exception as he prayed to God:

Purge me with hyssop and I shall be clean;
Wash me and I shall be whiter than snow. *Psalm 51:9*

What should we do when we feel unclean and heartsick? How can we show that we are truly and sincerely sorry for what we have done?

8   What kind of faults did the Psalmist mean when he said:
Clear Thou me from hidden faults.   *Psalm 19:13*

9   What did the Psalmist mean when he prayed:
So teach us to number our days,
That we may get us a heart of wisdom.   *Psalm 90:12*
How can we number our days to achieve a heart of wisdom?

THINGS TO DO

1   Read Psalm 15 for the 11 requirements of a truly religious person.

2   Look up the following references in the Psalms; then discuss in class, or write an essay on, the relationship of the Psalms to the teachings of the Prophets:
Psalms 33:5; 37:3; 37:27–28; 82:3–4; 86:11; 97:2; 101:5–7.

3   Which of the following Psalms apply to:
The words of a fool
On returning the Torah to the ark
God's time
The fate of the wicked
Consideration for the poor
Psalms 90:4; 37:20; 14:1; 41:2; 19:8–10.

4   Read Psalm 121:1–4. Why do lofty mountains inspire people with reverence for God? If there are any mountain-climbers in your congregation or community, interview them about their reactions to Psalm 121.

5   Arrange a visit to a planetarium to view the moon and the stars. Then write an essay on your reactions. Tell why the sight of the heavens fills us with reverence for God.

6   Interview your science teacher and ask how the study of astronomy demonstrates the wonder and order of God's universe.

7   Get acquainted with a Concordance, a reference book on the Bible. When you want to locate a specific quotation from the Psalms, or any part of the Bible, look up a word, or verse, in *Cruden's Complete*

Concordance. Under that word you will find a list of all the chapters and verses in the Bible where that word appears.

Locate the following statements, and list their sources in the Bible:

a A rod of iron

b Out of the mouths of babes and sucklings

c I have set the Lord always before me

d Keep thy tongue from evil

e We went through fire and water

f As a tale that is told

g He that keepeth Israel

h May the words of my mouth and the meditations of my heart be acceptable unto Thee.

8 Write an essay on the modern meaning of Psalm 133:1:

Behold, how good and how pleasant it is
For brethren to dwell together in unity!

9 Imagine that you are writing a movie script. Tell of an imaginary situation where faith helped someone to fight his fears.

SELECTED QUOTATIONS

The Psalms in Human Life

Above the couch of David, according to Rabbinical tradition, there hung a harp. The midnight breeze, as it rippled over the strings, made such music that the poet King was constrained to rise from his bed, and till dawn flushed the eastern skies he wedded words to the strains. The poetry of that tradition is condensed in the saying that the Book of Psalms contains the whole music of the heart of man, swept by the hand of his Maker. In it are gathered the lyrical burst of his tenderness, the moan of his penitence, the pathos of his sorrow, the triumph of his victory, the despair of his defeat, the firmness of his confidence, the rapture of his assured hope.

. . . They alone have known no limitations to a particular age, country or form of faith. In the Psalms the vast hosts of suffering humanity have found the deepest expression of their hopes and fears.

R. E. PROTHRO

A Whole Drama of Humanity

In the Psalms are collected "sunrise and sunset, birth and death, promise and fulfillment, a whole drama of humanity."

HEINRICH HEINE

What Is Man?

Man—what is he in this God-filled world? What is his place in this throng of creatures of God, this choir of servants of the Lord? . . . Can he be born only to take? . . . to revel in lavish plenty or to starve in misery, but not to work? . . . not to fill any place, nor fulfill any purpose, but to let all end in himself? The world and all which is therein serves God. Is it conceivable that man alone should only serve himself? No! Your consciousness pronounces you as does the Torah. "An image of God." That is what man should be. Only when working out some end canst thou know God in love and righteousness; to work out ends of righteousness and love art thou called; not merely to enjoy or suffer. All which thou possessest, spirit, body, wealth, every ability and every power, they are means of activity; to promote and preserve the world were they given in love and righteousness.

The Nineteen Letters of Ben Uziel
RABBI SAMSON RAPHAEL HIRSCH

If I Ascend Unto Heaven

During a raid on Schweinfurst during World War II, one of our bombers, *Battlin' Bobbie*, was hit, and two of her engines were knocked out . . . For five hundred miles, the bomber hedge-hopped over trees, roof tops and enemy pillboxes . . . All the time as the plane limped along her crew kept praying the two smoking engines wouldn't blow up . . . When they finally reached home and the perspiring pilot climbed out of the ship, his comment was, "We made a chapel out of that airplane today."

The Treasury of the Psalms

The Book of Psalms contains almost every great religious idea which grew up in Israel. Some of the psalms are epic poetry. There are psalms which express the ethical idealism of the prophets (Psalm 15). Some psalms express the mood of study and a love of wisdom characteristic of the Book of Proverbs. Other psalms echo the great historical vision with its idea of the role of God as the Guide of human destiny as expressed in Deuteronomy and in the historical books. The Book of Psalms is an epitome of all the nobler religious ideas developed in Israel.

SOLOMON FREEHOF, *The Book of Psalms*

SUGGESTED READINGS

Cohen, M. I., *Pathways Through The Bible*, pp. 421–422.
Bloch, Chayim, *The Golem.*
Freehof, Solomon, *The Book of Psalms.*
Universal Jewish Encyclopedia, Vol. 9, pp. 15–19.
The Holy Scriptures, Jewish Publication Society Edition, Psalms.

7

THE VOICE OF WISDOM

The Ethics of the Book of Proverbs

At Home

"You're all against me! All of you! You treat me like a baby and never let me do anything. Someday I'll leave home and live my own life, and nobody will be able to stop me!" Sobbing, Esther jumped up from her chair and ran out of the dining room.

There was silence at the table until Jackie said: "Whew! There goes my atomic sister again. She's always blowing up! I was only teasing when I kidded her about . . ."

"That will do, Jackie," Father interrupted. "You had no right to say what you did, and from now on I want you to stop teasing your sister."

"But, Dad, I was only . . ."

"I know you were only teasing, but I'm not going to have these scenes at the dinner-table, and I mean it!"

Lester Greenberg turned to his wife. "Martha, what's been going on here? Esther's been pouting and tensed-up for days. Have you two been fighting?"

Mrs. Greenberg said angrily, "Esther resents everything I say to her. I know she's at a difficult age, but I don't know what to do with her any more. Whatever I do, whatever I say, throws her into a tantrum. I'm going to my room and lie down for awhile. The cake is in the kitchen. You can get your own dessert."

Mrs. Greenberg went to her room, leaving Mr. Greenberg and Jackie at the table. Mr. Greenberg picked up his fork, and then put it down again. "I'm not very hungry either, Jackie," he said. "Maybe I'll finish my dinner later. I'm going out to the porch and read the evening paper."

"O.K., Dad," Jackie muttered through a mouthful of food, and then reached over for another piece of fried chicken.

Better Is a Dry Morsel

We can easily understand why Jackie Greenberg listened with such unusual interest as Rabbi Mayer began the lesson on the Book of Proverbs:

> *Better is a dry morsel and quietness therewith, than a house full of feasting with strife.*   *Proverbs 17:1*

Jackie remembered the loud voices, the angry looks, the tension and bitterness of the night before. The family had gathered at the table for dinner, and then it began. First Esther left the table. Then Mother, and finally Father.

Jackie asked himself: "What if we had been too poor to afford that delicious dinner? Instead of having fried chicken, potato salad, a jello mold and a good dessert, what if there was only a dry crust of bread on every plate? But what if there had been laughter, love, and harmony?" He visualized a family picture: Esther seated at the table, telling the family about her experiences of the day, her eyes sparkling as she laughed about a funny incident. Mother listened attentively, with a happy look on her face. Father grinned at the story, eating his food with relish. After a difficult day at work, he had come home to love and laughter and, above all, peace.

Jackie sighed as a platter of fried chicken faded away before his eyes. He liked fried chicken, but he also liked what he saw in this family picture. The wise author of the proverb might have been talking about his own family when he said, *Better is a dry morsel and quietness therewith, than a house full of feasting with strife.*

The Little Sanctuary

Rabbi Mayer said: "We believe that the Still, Small Voice can be heard in the home, just as it is heard in the synagogue or temple. As a matter of fact, in Jewish tradition we have called the home a *Mikdosh M'at*, a little sanctuary.

"We would not think of walking into a sanctuary of God and using profane language, shouting, yelling or quarreling. We remember the inscription written on the ark: *Know Before Whom You Stand*. Realizing that we stand in the presence of God, we turn our thoughts to high ideals. A spirit of reverence comes over us. God is near, watching what we do and hearing what we say.

"It is because we believe that God's presence is in our home too, that we call it 'a little sanctuary.' That is why we should think of our home as a holy place. In many of our homes there is a *mezuzah* on the doorpost. God's name is on the *mezuzah—Shaddai*, God Almighty. This is to remind us that when we enter our homes, we are entering into the presence of God, and that whatever we do and whatever we say should be pleasing to God. Just as we have prayers and ceremonies in the synagogue, so we have prayers and ceremonies in the home: our morning and evening prayers, the blessing before meals, the lighting of the candles, the Kiddush on the Sabbath, the observance of Hanukkah, Purim, and Passover. All of this brings God closer to us, and brings us closer to God in thankfulness and joy.

"The home has been a sanctuary in another sense, too. During times of persecution, the Jew returned to his home to find a sanctuary from the pain and hurt that others had inflicted. In his home, he was like a high priest. His wife was queen, and his children princes and princesses. Here he was at peace. He could say his prayers and worship his God according to his faith and his conscience. The Still, Small Voice speaking to him in the sanctuary of the home helped him to gain strength and courage to go on, to meet evil with quiet dignity, to practice justice, truth, and deeds of lovingkindness.

The Sanctity of the Family

"And so the Jewish home was not a castle. Rather it was a sanctuary. In it, members of the family drew close to each other in tenderness and love. To make the home a sanctuary became a part of our religious faith, and a special phrase became part of the everyday vocabulary of the Jew. The phrase was *taharath mishpocho*, the purity, or holiness, of the family. It meant that Jews practiced the teachings of Judaism in the home as well as in the synagogue, the marketplace, and in their daily work. It meant that the members of a Jewish family obeyed the Still, Small Voice through devotion, unselfish love, loyalty, and above all by living together in peace, quiet, and holiness."

Terry raised his hand. "Is that still a requirement today, Rabbi? Does it apply to modern Jews, or is it something that was only true in the past?"

"It is still an important part of our Jewish faith today, Terry," answered Rabbi Mayer. "When I attend interfaith meetings, someone invariably comments on the beauty and love of Jewish family life. That doesn't mean that you have to be Jewish to have these things. We don't have any monopoly on love and holiness. But this is more or less characteristic of Jews—to be a closely-knit family, and to show love and loyalty to each other at all times. The proverb, *Better is a dry morsel and quietness therewith, than a house full of feasting with strife*, reminds us of the holiness of the family. It tells us that if we listen, we will hear the Still, Small Voice speaking to us in the little sanctuary, our home."

WHAT DO YOU THINK?

1 What do you think about Esther's behavior? How do you think she might have handled the situation?

2 How could a family council after dinner have helped the Greenbergs with their problems?

3 Would Jewish home ceremonies help bring peace to the Greenberg household? How?

4 What is meant by the sanctity of Jewish family life?

5 How would you explain the traditional devotion and closeness of the Jewish family?

6 In what way does the sanctity of the Jewish family account for the low rate of juvenile delinquency among Jewish boys and girls?

7 How can Judaism help make your home a little sanctuary?

After the class had discussed these questions, Rabbi Mayer said: "Don't ever think that the Still, Small Voice speaks only to great and holy men, to prophets, kings, and sages. Don't think it is only heard on mountain tops, in a burning bush, or in some miracle of nature. Ordinary men and women, boys and girls, can hear the Still, Small Voice in the normal aspects of daily life.

"The practical wisdom of the Book of Proverbs tries to teach

each of us to listen to the Still, Small Voice in our homes, at work, in our daily routines. The Proverbs were not written for past generations alone. They apply to us too, to the way we act and the way we live today. The Book of Proverbs can help us win the biggest battle of our lives.

The Biggest Fight of Your Life

"The Book of Proverbs tells us: *Envy not the man of violence, and choose none of his ways* (Prov. 3:31). But often we envy the man of violence. We tend to look up to people who are big, tough, and strong, and sometimes we want to be like them. We admire the wrestlers we see on television, men of tremendous physical strength. A heavyweight boxing championship fight draws huge crowds who want to watch men battle for fame and money. We honor our military leaders, men who have led us to victory in war. It is thrilling to read of their courage and patriotism.

"But there is another kind of strength, and another kind of victory. We don't always give medals for it. And yet this is the very strength you will need to win your big fight.

"Who is the opponent? How can you win this fight? The Book of Proverbs gives the answer. But first you must ask yourself: Do you control your temper, or does your temper control you?

Losing Your Temper

"When a baby is angry or upset, he screams. He cannot reason, or understand why things happen. He cannot wait for whatever he wants. As the baby grows, he often has temper tantrums. The time or place doesn't matter. The child can't control his temper. It controls him.

"But as the child matures, he learns that he can control his temper. Sometimes he gets what he wants by losing his temper. Sometimes he gets what he doesn't want—punishment, a spanking. Then one day he begins to try to control his rage and anger.

"Very often we hear boys and girls say: 'I have a terrible temper. I would like to control it, but there's nothing I can do about it!' Isn't it surprising, though, how we control our tempers when we really want to? For example, the boy who tells his parents 'I can't control my temper,' finds that he is quite able to control it if another boy picks a fight, and the other boy happens to be bigger and tougher than he. A girl will be able to control her anger to stay in the good graces of someone she admires. Oh yes, we can control our tempers—if we really want to.

"The mature person has learned to control his temper. He has developed the kind of strong character that enables him to conquer himself. This is not an easy thing to do. Many people never achieve it. Just as an athlete must train his body and coordinate his movements, so a person must train his character, exert the control of reason over his words and actions.

"The Book of Proverbs put it this way:

> *He that is slow to anger is better than the mighty;*
> *And he that ruleth his spirit than he that taketh a city.*
>
> *Proverbs 16:32*

"Doesn't this tell you the identity of the greatest opponent you will ever have?" Rabbi Mayer asked. "Doesn't this give you a clue to the biggest fight of your life? Mighty warriors are not the only heroes. There are those who have learned to conquer themselves. Let me tell you about a modern hero and how he won a great battle."

Courage in the Dark

The two boys wrestled vigorously on the mat. One was blind in one eye. But he never let this keep him from participating in sports. Perhaps he even struggled harder to win.

Suddenly, accidentally, his friend's elbow jabbed him in his good eye. His vision blurred, a red haze glowed, and then everything was black. The 16-year-old boy was rushed to the hospital. After long consultations with specialists, the verdict was given. He was hopelessly, totally blind.

At first he was bitter. Why had this happened? For the rest of his life, he would be helpless, a burden on his friends, needing them to guide him through the darkness of life. What could he do? How could he become self-sufficient, how could he earn his own living, go where he wanted to go, live a normal life without being an object of pity? He had to find a way.

When he was 19, a friend told him about an article in the *Saturday Evening Post.* It described a wonderful new project for the blind. There was a special school in Switzerland where dogs were trained to lead the sightless. But the men and women had to be trained too. They had to learn to accept their dogs as friends, and to have enough faith in themselves to walk down stairways, cross busy streets, led only by a dog. The dogs were to be the very eyes of the blind.

"Perhaps this is the way," he thought. He sent a cablegram to Switzerland. Mrs. Eustice, the head of the school, replied that the school would accept him for training. With new hope, with the possibility of a new life opening before him, he decided to make the trip. His relatives offered to accompany him, but he crossed the ocean alone. His independence had begun. Soon he was enrolled in the school, its only pupil at the time.

After months of gruelling training, he was ready to go out with his dog, Kiss. He renamed him Buddy. Buddy was keen, sensitive, alert to every touch of his master's hand on the harness. This harness was their means of communication. When Buddy did something wrong, his master would say "phooie!" When Buddy was particularly swift in obeying, he was praised with the words, "Good, Buddy, Good, Buddy!" Man and dog became devoted friends. The young man was no longer helpless and dependent. He could go wherever he wished, with Buddy to guide him there in safety.

Now this young man decided to help others like himself. He would establish a school in the United States where the blind could find trained dogs to serve as their eyes. With the help of friends, Morris Frank—for that was his name—organized a school in Nashville, Tennessee. The school failed. But he made new plans, tried again. Through hard work and unfailing effort, his school at Morristown, New Jersey, became famous throughout the world.

These wonderful dogs who were the eyes of their masters were given a special name, a name taken from the Book of Proverbs, Chapter 20, Verse 12.

> *The hearing ear, and the seeing eye,*
> *The Lord hath made even both of them.*

Whenever you see a man or woman with a Seeing Eye Dog, remember this verse from Proverbs. And think of the courage of

Morris Frank, a modern hero who learned to see in the dark, and thereby won the biggest battle of his life. When he conquered his fear, he conquered himself.

The Hearing Ear and the Seeing Eye

Rabbi Mayer closed his notebook, and said: *"The hearing ear, and the seeing eye, the Lord hath made even both of them.* What noble use was made of this statement from the Book of Proverbs! God gave us the blessing of hearing, that we might listen to the Still, Small Voice. He blessed us with vision that we might see where we walk. And we have the power to choose our directions: toward good or evil, selfishness or unselfishness, wrongdoing or righteousness."

Dianne raised her hand. "Rabbi, that reminds me of the prayer you read when you put the Torah back into the Ark: *It is a tree of life. . . ."*

"You are right, Dianne," said Rabbi Mayer. "The prayer concludes: *its ways are ways of pleasantness, and all its paths are peace.* That too comes from the Book of Proverbs, Chapter 3:17. You see, the wisdom of the proverbs teaches us that we find happiness and peace by obeying the Torah and following the ways of God. Sometimes, however, people have other ideas of how to find happiness, as we will see in the following story.

The Secret of Happiness

"An ancient Persian king dreamed one night of finding true happiness. The next day he summoned the wise men of his kingdom and demanded to know how he might achieve his heart's desire. And the wise men told him: 'Find a happy man, and wear his shirt, O King, and you shall witness the fulfillment of your dreams.' So the monarch sent his messengers throughout the realm in search of a happy man. The search continued for many months. The months extended into years, while the weary messengers traveled through the kingdom, each hoping to be the one to bring back the coveted shirt, the shirt that would enable the king to find happiness. At last, they found a happy man—but he was so poor that, alas, he had no shirt!

"From the beginning of time," said Rabbi Mayer, "man has sought the secret of happiness. Some thought it was power; others believed it was love, or health, or fame, or riches.

"Today some people like to think that money is the secret of happiness. They devote a lifetime to the search for wealth. But after acquiring it, they learn that they must still continue their search for happiness. What, then, is the secret of happiness—love, health, fame, power or riches?

"The Book of Proverbs offers several ways to achieve happiness: One writer believed:

> *Happy is the man that findeth wisdom,*
> *and the man that obtaineth understanding.*
> *For the merchandise of it is better than the merchandise of*
> *silver,*
> *And the gain thereof than fine gold.*
>
>   *Proverbs 3:13–14*

"A second writer offered another formula for happiness. He believed that those who obey God's commandments and follow the ways of God find true happiness.

> *Happy are they that keep my ways.*
>
>   *Proverbs 8:32*

"Have you ever carried a grudge?" asked the Rabbi. "Before you answer, consider this statement from the Book of Proverbs and pay close attention to the story of Eleanor and Shirley."

> *Hatred stirreth up strifes,*
> *But love covereth all transgressions.*   *Proverbs 10:12*

Carrying a Grudge

When Eleanor was eleven years old, her mother spoke out in opposition to sororities at a Temple Parent-Teacher meeting. Three years later, Eleanor's friends were being pledged to sororities and Eleanor hoped she would be invited to join too. But many of the girls felt that Eleanor should not be pledged because of her mother's strong stand against the sorority system.

Reba, Eleanor's dearest friend, argued that Eleanor had a right to belong, no matter what her mother thought. Then Shirley spoke up. "I don't think we should pledge Eleanor. It would hurt the sorority. After all, her mother has talked against us all over town. What's more, Eleanor is awfully stuck-up and high hat. I don't like her."

The girls agreed not to pledge Eleanor. Reba was furious, walked out of the meeting, and returned her pledge pin the very next day.

Eleanor was very upset when she learned about the sorority's decision. She was grateful for Reba's loyalty. But she vowed that someday she would find a way to hurt Shirley as deeply as Shirley had hurt her.

A few months later, Shirley felt genuinely sorry for what she had done. She proposed Eleanor's name for membership in the sorority, and this time Eleanor was invited to join the group. But she refused. Shirley then went to Eleanor and apologized for her past actions; she hoped Eleanor would forgive her and that they would be friends. Eleanor said, "Forget it. It wasn't that important to me." Shirley believed her.

But Eleanor didn't forget. Every night she prayed, "Dear God, help me get even with Shirley."

Six months later, her chance came. Shirley had applied for a summer camp scholarship in Maine. The camp director was a close friend of Eleanor's parents. Shirley had to submit the names of two former campers as character references, and Eleanor offered to write in her behalf.

Then Eleanor wrote a cruel letter, saying that Shirley was selfish, mean, of poor character. She hoped Shirley's application would be refused, and that the scholarship would go to a more deserving applicant. At last Eleanor had gotten even.

The camp director compared Eleanor's letter with others from the rabbi, the school principal, and Girl Scout executive. All of them testified to Shirley's fine character. The director decided to give Shirley the scholarship.

When Eleanor learned about this, she cried herself to sleep. She was more bitter than ever. And when Shirley learned of what Eleanor had tried to do, she refused to speak to Eleanor ever again.

Rabbi Mayer said: "Hate creates strife. A grudge becomes a heavy burden; we cannot carry it for long without hurting ourselves. It boomerangs; it fills us with unhappiness. Eleanor's grudge harmed her more than it did Shirley. But kindness and love enrich us. They bring us very close to the mystery of the Still, Small Voice; they contain the secret of happiness.

Love Covers All Transgressions

"In an ancient Hebrew book that has come down to us from Maccabean times, the *Testament of the Twelve Patriarchs*, we read:

> *Love ye one another from the heart, and if a man sin against thee, cast forth the poison of hate and speak peaceably to him. If he confess and repent, forgive him. But if he be shameless and persist in his wrongdoing, even so forgive him from the heart and leave to God the avenging. Beware of hatred, for it works lawlessness, even against the Lord*

*Himself, for it will not hear the words of the command-
ment concerning the love of one's neighbor. Love would
quicken even the dead, and would call back them that are
condemned to die, but hatred would slay the living.*

"The rabbis once taught, 'He who has a forgiving spirit is himself forgiven. Whosoever does not persecute them that persecute
him, whosoever suffers wrong in silence and requites it not, they are
deemed friends of God.'"

I'm Not That Noble

After class, Burton and Susan walked home together. Burton
wasn't impressed with the idea of so much forgiveness and love.
"That's all right for saints," he said, "but not for people today.
When somebody hurts you, you've got to fight back. This business of suffering in silence isn't for me. I'm not that noble. Just
imagine the kind of world where people don't stand up for themselves, where everybody loves everybody else, no matter what they
do or say. It just isn't practical."

"I wish I could live in such a world," answered Susan. "Look at
the world we do have—suspicion, war, hatred, the atom bomb.
Nations are grabbing and greedy. Millions are starving. Just how
practical is your way, Burton?"

"Just a minute," she said as Burton tried to interrupt. "I'm not
through. Maybe the trouble with our world is that we haven't really
tried to live the religious way. People always call those ideals im-
practical and unrealistic. We've tried hatred and vengeance, but
we've never tried love, forgiveness, and unselfishness."

"Will you let me get a word in?" asked Burton. "You keep talking about the world, and what this world would be like if people
loved each other and suffered wrongs in silence. That's easy for
you to say, but what about *you*? Are *you* big enough to forgive

people who wrong you? Can *you* love people who try to hurt you? Can *you* show kindness to people who hate you?"

"No, I can't, but . . ."

"There. You see it doesn't work in real life. That stuff is for writers, dreamers and religious teachers, for lessons and sermons. Look at yourself. You're angry right now. Why aren't you calm and peaceful and good-natured about what I'm saying, even though you don't agree with me?"

Susan knew she was going to cry in a minute. She tried to hold the tears back, but her voice broke into a sob. Burton had made her angry, and she wanted to show him that it was better not to be angry. She was arguing for love, and yet she was so annoyed at Burton that she wanted to slap him. She was so upset that she couldn't keep from crying.

When Burton saw that he had goaded Susan to tears, he was sorry. He tried to soothe her: "Don't take it so hard, Susan. We were only having a friendly argument. I didn't mean to make you cry. I'm sorry. Believe me, I'm sorry."

In a few minutes Susan was able to laugh. "I'm acting like a baby. I always want to kick myself when I cry like that. But listen, Burton. I didn't mean that I'm so perfect, and I didn't say I was big enough or good enough to forgive those who wrong me or love those who hate me. But that's the way I'd like to be, and that's what I'm going to try to be. Maybe I won't succeed, but I'm going to try my best to forgive those who hurt me. I believe it's wrong to ask God to forgive us if we don't try to forgive others. What's more, I believe that hating hurts us more than it does the people we hate. It's like filling our bodies with poison."

Burton was quiet while Susan spoke. Then he said: "I don't know about forgiving others, but I'll tell you this. It's true that when you hurt others, you hurt yourself. When I saw how upset you were, I felt miserable and upset too. Even though it seemed I had won the argument, I didn't get any fun or enjoyment out of winning. Suppose we call a truce and stop off at the Sweet Shoppe for an ice cream soda. After that, if it isn't too late, we can work on the assignment Rabbi Mayer gave us. What was it? I think it had something to do with reading a list of selected proverbs to see whether they were practical and could be applied to the problems of daily life."

Susan opened her purse and took out a mirror. She looked at herself, and then brushed her hair in place with her hand. After that she said: "I'm ready now. Let's apply an ice cream soda to the problem of an empty stomach. That's the most practical thing I can think of right now."

APPLYING THE WISDOM OF PROVERBS

Read each proverb and discuss in class the practical application of each statement. How can these teachings help us solve the mystery of the Still, Small Voice?

> *1 Pride goeth before destruction*
> *And a haughty spirit before a fall.*
>
> *Proverbs 16:18*

> *2 A false witness shall not be unpunished,*
> *And he that breatheth forth lies shall not escape.*
>
> *Proverbs 19:5*

> *3 Whoso keepeth his mouth and his tongue,*
> *Keepeth his soul from troubles.*
>
> *Proverbs 21:23*

> *4 Answer not a fool according to his folly,*
> *Lest thou also be like unto him.*
>
> *Proverbs 26:4*

> *5 Boast not thyself of tomorrow,*
> *For thou Knoweth not what a day may bring forth.*
>
> *Proverbs 27:1*

6 *Hast thou found honey?*
Eat so much as is sufficient for thee,
Lest thou be filled therewith, and vomit it.

Proverbs 25:16

7 *Whoso diggeth a pit shall fall therein,*
And he that rolleth a stone, it shall return upon him.

Proverbs 26:27

8 *A tranquil heart is the life of the flesh,*
But envy is the rottenness of the bones.

Proverbs 14:30

9 *Whoso loveth knowledge loveth correction:*
But he that is brutish hateth reproof.

Proverbs 12:1

10 *Let not kindness and truth forsake thee,*
Bind them about thy neck,
Write them upon the table of thy heart:
So shalt thou find grace and good favour
In the sight of God and man.

Proverbs 3:3–4

11 *Be not wise in thine own eyes;*
Revere the Lord and depart from evil.

Proverbs 3:7

12 *Withhold not good from him to whom it is due,*
When it is in the power of thy hand to do it.

Proverbs 3:27

13 *A friend loveth at all times,*
And a brother is born for adversity.

Proverbs 17:17

14 *He that giveth answer before he heareth,*
It is folly and confusion unto him.

Proverbs 18:13

15 *A good name is rather to be chosen than great riches,*
And loving favor rather than silver and gold.

Proverbs 22:1

16 As a ring of gold in a swine's snout,
   So is a fair woman that turneth aside from discretion.

                                   Proverbs 11:22

17 The fear of the Lord is to hate evil;
   Pride, and arrogancy, and the evil way,
   And the froward mouth, do I hate.

                                   Proverbs 8:13

18 Trust in the Lord with all thy heart,
   And lean not upon thine own understanding,
   In all thy ways acknowledge Him,
   And He will direct thy paths.

                                   Proverbs 3:5–6

QUESTIONS FOR DISCUSSION

1   The late Rabbi J. H. Hertz, the former Chief Rabbi of England, once wrote:

Holiness is thus attained not by flight from the world, nor by monk-like renunciation of human relationships of family or station, but by the spirit in which we fulfil the obligations of life in its simplest and commonest details: in this way—by doing justly, loving mercy, and walking humbly with our God—is everyday life transfigured.

What did he mean?

2   To what extent is the wisdom of the Book of Proverbs Jewish? Do the sayings apply to Christians and Mohammedans as well as to Jews?

3   Can you tell of experiences in your life or in the life of another, proving that the proverb is correct when it states:

   A soft answer turneth away wrath,
   But a grievous word stirreth up anger.

                                   Proverbs 15:1

4   How does history prove that:

   Righteousness exalteth a nation,
   But sin is a reproach to any people.

                                   Proverbs 14:34

5   What is the meaning of this statement:
The fear of the Lord is the beginning of knowledge;
But the foolish despise wisdom and discipline.

Proverbs 1:7

6   In Proverbs 10:27, we read:
The fear of the Lord prolongeth days;
But the years of the wicked shall be shortened.

How can reverence for God prolong life?
In what way does the wicked person shorten his life?

7   What did the writer of Proverbs mean when he wrote:
Every wise woman buildeth her house;
But the foolish plucketh it down with her own hands.

Proverbs 14:1

8   Hayyim Schauss, in his book, *The Jewish Festivals*, writes:
Life in a Jewish home of several centuries ago was full of tenderness
and piety. The relationship between man and wife was tender and true,
as was the relationship between parents and children. This spirit was
evidenced especially on the Sabbath and festivals.

On Friday night, after all work had been put aside, the entire family
gathered about the father, the head of the house, and presented a picture
of hominess and warmth.

Is this true of Jewish family life today? If not, what has happened to
change the character of Jewish family life? How can it be restored to
what it was?

9   A modern Jewish writer, Meyer Waxman, stated that "there is no
religion or nation in which the family occupies such an important place
as in Judaism." Do you agree or disagree? Why?

10   Read Ecclesiastes, Chapter 12, Verses 13–14. What is meant by
"For this is the whole man"?

11   Do people generally feel better or worse after "getting even"
with an enemy?

12   Rabbi Julius Gordon wrote a book called *Pity the Persecutor.*

What do you think he meant by that title? Do you think a persecutor should be pitied? Why?

THINGS TO DO

1 *Go to the Ant, thou sluggard: consider her ways, and be wise.*

Proverbs 6:6

Study the habits of the ant, and then suggest what we as human beings can learn from the ant.

2 Look up the meaning and significance of the Apocrypha. Why do you think it was not included in the Bible?

3 Read Chapter II of the "Wisdom of Solomon," in the Apocrypha. How would someone your own age express those same thoughts in the language of today?

4 Read the story of "Bel and the Dragon" in the Apocrypha. Re-write it as a modern detective story, pointing out today's idols, or modern objects of worship.

5 Examine the Book of Proverbs: what are the seven things God dislikes? What are the four things of wonder?

6 The Book of Ecclesiastes was almost omitted from the Bible, although it is regarded as a part of Wisdom Literature. Can you explain why it was regarded with suspicion? Read Chapter I and write your reactions.

7 Which of the following Proverbs apply to:

Greediness	The talebearer
Honesty in business	Drunkards and gluttons
Kindness to animals	Boastfulness

A nagging woman

Proverbs 20:19; 27:15; 12:10; 11:1; 27:1–2; 23:30–35; 15:27.

8 Compare St. Paul's Epistle to the Romans, 12:20, with Proverbs 25:21.

9 Compare Proverbs 16:8; 21:3; 21:13; 22:22–23 with the teachings of the Prophets.

10 Write an original story, using this verse from Proverbs as the theme.

> *Treasures of wickedness profit nothing;*
> *But righteousness delivereth from death.*
>
>   *Proverbs 10:2*

11 Read Proverbs 31:10–31; then write an essay comparing the ideal Jewish wife and mother of Proverbs with our standards for an ideal Jewish wife and mother today.

12 Read Proverbs 31:10–31; then compare the attitude toward women as indicated in Proverbs with the Arab's attitude and treatment of women. Use the library and find the references that will help you.

13 Read Proverbs 31:10–31; then do research on the status of women in the state of Israel today. In an essay, list the new rights gained by the Arab women who live in Israel.

14 Four members of the class should write 3 socio-dramas. These are situations to test how we would behave in certain situations, and how we would react to certain problems. The socio-dramas are enacted by members of the class with the assistance of some adults.

Example: A boy and girl play brother and sister at home. The boy says that parents show preference for sister. The girl says that parents favor brother. They quarrel. Their parents come in. The children ask mother and father: "Which of us is your favorite? Please don't tell us that you love both of us the same!" The parents then react to these statements and talk to son and daughter. (Class gives reaction after socio-drama is completed.)

Example: A girl tells her mother that she has been invited to a school party by a Christian boy. She doesn't particularly like him, but didn't want him to think that because she was Jewish she wouldn't go out with him. She asks her mother: "Was I right in accepting his invitation?" The member of the class playing the part of the mother then responds. After the socio-drama is completed, members of the class tell what they believe the mother should have said.

15 The Book of Proverbs sets forth a basis for etiquette. Copy the following quotations:

Proverbs 25:17; 6:12–13; 16:24; 15:17; 20:9; 25:9; 4:25; 11:16.

Then write your own code of etiquette for youth today.

SELECTED QUOTATIONS

A Guide to Happy Living

The Book of Proverbs . . . deals out practical counsel for earthly happiness: if one is righteous, one will be happy. Even the definition of happiness is practical and earthy: happiness is long life, good health, wealth and contented family living. The books therefore are merely practical counsel as to how to attain success in life.

SOLOMON FREEHOF, *Preface to Scripture*

Vengeance and Forgiveness

He that revengeth shall find vengeance from the Lord, and he will surely keep his sins in remembrance. Forgive thy neighbor the hurt that he hath done unto thee, so shall thy sins also be forgiven when thou prayest. One man beareth hatred against another, and doth he seek pardon from the Lord? He showeth no mercy to a man which is like himself: yet doth he ask forgiveness of his own sins . . . Remember the commandments and bear no malice to thy neighbor.

Ecclesiasticus 28:1–7

Thou Shalt Not Hate Thy Brother in Thy Heart

It is forbidden for an Israelite to hate his neighbor; for it is written: "Thou shalt not hate thy brother in thine heart." (Lev. 19:17) And we find that it was the hatred of the brothers for Joseph which brought our ancestors into the slavery of Egypt . . . Our Rabbis have taught: "Thou shalt not hate thy brother." Perhaps by this might be understood: "Thou shalt not wound him, thou shalt not quarrel with him, thou shalt commit no outrage against him." It is for this reason that the prophet adds: "Thou shalt not hate thy brother *in thine heart*," in order to make clear that it is not permitted to carry hatred toward any one within one's self, even if no outward expression is given to it. . . .

GAON ACHAI SHABCHA

Defraud Not the Poor

My son, defraud not the poor of his living, and make not the needy eyes to wait long. Make not a hungry soul sorrowful; neither provoke a man in his distress. Add not more trouble to a heart that is vexed; and defer not to give to him that is in need. Reject not the supplication of the afflicted; neither turn away thy face from a poor man. Turn not away thine eye from the needy, and give him none occasion to curse thee; for if he curse thee in the bitterness of his soul, his prayer shall be heard of Him that made him.

Ecclesiasticus, Chapter 4

Honoring Parents

Whoso honoureth his father maketh an atonement for his sins: and he that honoureth his mother is as one that layeth up treasure. Whoso honoureth his father shall have joy of his own children; and when he maketh his prayer, he shall be heard . . . Honour thy father and mother both in word and deed, that a blessing may come upon thee from them. For the blessing of the father establisheth the houses of children; but the curse of the mother rooteth out foundations.

Ecclesiasticus, Chapter 3

The Genius of the Jewish Home

The genius of the Jewish home has ever been to combine sincere piety of worship and observance, with genuine gaiety which grows out of personal relationships grounded in the deep roots of character. A religious program, experienced in common by the entire household, does actually draw husband and wife into closer harmony, and does actually "turn the hearts of the parents to the children, and the hearts of the children to the parents." The atmosphere is one that promotes the fullest spiritual as well as cultural development of each individual.

Planning a Jewish Home,
Central Conference of American Rabbis

SUGGESTED READINGS

Cohen, M. J., *Pathways Through the Bible*, pp. 447–458.

Freehof, Solomon, *Preface to Scripture*, pp. 209–214.

Markowitz, Samuel, *Leading a Jewish Life in the Modern World*, Chapter VI.

Planning a Jewish Home, Central Conference of American Rabbis.

Radin, Max, *The Life of the People in Biblical Times*, Chapter III, The Household and Its Members.

Universal Jewish Encyclopedia, Proverbs, Volume 9, pp. 7–10.

Waxman, Meyer, *A History of Jewish Literature*, Vol. I, pp. 1–44, Apocryphal and Apocalyptic Literature.

8

THE VOICE OF THE FATHERS

Ethics of the Pirke Aboth

A Blackball for Rickey

"No, I will not! I don't care what you say, Jimmy, I'm not going to have Rickey Ruhlberg in my club! There's something wrong with that guy. He's just not like the other kids, and I don't want him!" Marvin started to leave the school yard.

His friend Jimmy took two long strides to catch up with him. "I think you're too tough on Rickey," he said. "Maybe there's a reason for his being different."

"What reason could there be?" questioned Marvin. "When we all go to a show, he says he can't go with us. When we want to go out for a coke, he says he doesn't like cokes. He talks funny, too. Like he's got a mouthful of mush. He never does anything the gang does. That's why I'm going to blackball him when his name comes up at the meeting."

Jimmy thought for a moment, and then said: "It's hard to argue with you, Marv. You're right when you say that he's different, but maybe there's a reason. Rabbi Mayer knows his family quite well. Suppose we ask the Rabbi what he thinks about it? What do you say?"

Marvin hesitated, "I don't know. What could Rabbi Mayer tell us to make us like him? I don't know . . ."

Sensing the uncertainty in Marvin's voice, Jimmy asked: "What have we got to lose? Come on, Marv."

Marvin agreed reluctantly, and the two boys entered the temple and asked to see the Rabbi. The Rabbi said he would be glad to talk to them, and they walked up the stairs to his study.

In the Rabbi's Study

After the Rabbi had listened to Marvin's reasons for wanting to blackball Rickey Ruhlberg, he walked to the bookshelves and selected a small volume. He turned a few pages and then, holding up the book, he said, "Boys, this is a tractate of the Mishnah called *Pirke Aboth*. The popular name for it is *The Sayings*, or *the Ethics, of the Fathers*. It appears in the prayerbook, too. Marvin, will you read this line?"

Marvin read:

> *Do not judge your neighbor until you are in his place.*

The Rabbi paused a moment, and said, "That's good advice, fellows. Why not try to follow it?"

"But what does that have to do with blackballing Rickey?" asked Marvin. "I don't want to hurt him, but he just wouldn't be a part of the club. He's too different."

"I understand how you feel, Marvin, and before I explain why I asked you to read that statement from the *Pirke Aboth*, let me tell you about another boy who was misjudged by his classmates.

The Boy with Long Hair

"This boy was scorned and ridiculed by his classmates because he wore his hair very long. He took the ridicule and badgering with quiet dignity and good humor. One day he went swimming with his friends. When he dived into the water, his long hair was swept back, and his classmates, eyes riveted upon him, saw with amazement that *the boy had no ears!* He had let his hair grow long to cover the ugly scars that should have been ears. He didn't want anyone to feel sorry for him, and so he accepted teasing about his hair rather than pity.

"The boys never meant to hurt him or judge him harshly. They just didn't know. That's why the rabbis taught: *Do not judge your neighbor until you are in his place.*"

"I see your point, Rabbi Mayer," said Marvin, "but what does it have to do with Rickey? Is there something wrong with him?"

"No, there's nothing wrong with Rickey," answered the Rabbi. "There's a great deal that's right and good about him. I want to tell you a few things about Rickey that may explain why he doesn't join in the fun with the other boys. He wouldn't tell you, but I don't think he will mind if I do.

"You say that he won't go to a show with you? Rickey's father isn't well—his eyesight is about gone—and he can't carry a full time job. So Rickey has a job as a delivery boy in the afternoons. His earnings help to pay the doctor's bills. That's why he won't go to a show with you.

"In the evenings, he reads to his father. That's why he doesn't go out with the boys. He never told you this because he doesn't like to advertise his problems. And about Rickey's speech—it's true that he doesn't speak clearly, but that's because he has a lateral lisp. He goes to a speech therapist on Saturday afternoons."

Marvin was silent, but Jimmy said, "Gosh, I never knew all this. Rickey never told us."

Marvin picked up the book and asked, "What did you say this book is called, Rabbi Mayer?"

"*Pirke Aboth*, the Sayings or Ethics of the Fathers."

Marvin spoke quietly, "Those rabbis knew what they were talking about, didn't they?" He scanned the page and read again, *Do not judge your neighbor until you are in his place.* If I were in Rickey's place, I might do the same things."

"Very likely you would, Marvin," agreed Rabbi Mayer. "That's why it's so dangerous to make snap judgments. Always give the other person the benefit of the doubt.

"In the next few class sessions, we'll look into the sayings of the rabbis and see if we can find other wise teachings, teachings that will help us apply Judaism to our everyday problems. Then we will all understand a little more about the Still, Small Voice."

Jimmy and Marvin left the Rabbi's study. "What about the black-ball, Marv?" Jimmy asked.

Marvin kicked at a stone on the pavement and said, "Forget it. I still don't like Rickey much, but as far as I'm concerned, he's in the club right now."

WHAT DO YOU THINK?

1 Should Rickey have told his classmates his reason for not joining in their activities? Was he right in not talking about his father's failing eyesight, or was he over-sensitive?

2 Do you think that Marvin had a right to blackball Rickey before he knew the facts? If you had been in Marvin's place, how would you have acted?

3 Is it right to blackball someone from a club or a private group, even though the person may be hurt by being rejected?

4 After learning the facts about Rickey, Marvin said that although he still didn't like him, he wouldn't keep him out of the club. Should he have blackballed him anyway?

A JUVENILE COURT CASE

A case came before the Juvenile Court. A boy of sixteen, Robert G., had been caught stealing. The judge was an understanding man and spoke kindly to Robert. But the boy was stubborn, surly, and disrespectful. His clothing was dirty and torn. The records showed that he had been in court twice before, once for stealing a car, and once for vandalism—throwing stones through a church window.

If you were the Juvenile Court judge, what would you do?

Write out your decision, and discuss it in class. Then study the following facts about Robert G., and write a new decision if the facts seem to warrant it.

The Case of Robert G.

Robert's parents, Raymond and Marie G., had police records. The father never held a job for very long. He spent his small earnings on liquor, coming home drunk. The neighbors reported that he cursed his wife and abused the child. He had spent three months at the County Hospital, receiving treatment for acute alcoholism. When Robert was ten years old, his father deserted the family. His whereabouts are unknown.

The mother worked for a while, and then began to leave town for days at a time. Neighbors took care of Robert. The Agency of Aid for Dependent Children tried to help. A social worker talked to Mrs. G., but reported her uncooperative. Robert was absent from school six months of the year. The truant officers took the case to court, and the authorities tried to place Robert in a foster home. But his mother would not give the necessary permission.

When Robert was 14 years old, his mother was convicted of shoplifting. She was given a suspended sentence. The Family Service Society was providing food and rent money for them. About this time, Robert was brought into court for stealing an automobile. He said he did it just for fun. Six months before his sixteenth birthday, he was brought into court again for throwing bricks through a church window. He said he didn't like the minister, and that church people were hypocrites.

Robert was examined by a physician who found that he was underweight, had a chronic skin disease and badly decayed teeth, and suffered from persistent colds. His intelligence was slightly below normal. A psychiatrist talked to Robert and reported that the boy believed everyone was against him.

If You Were in his Place

"Before we judge too harshly," said Rabbi Mayer, "we should pause and consider the teachings of the *Pirke Aboth*.

"Suppose the bases are loaded. The pitcher is doing his best. You yell: 'Strike him out!' The pitcher winds up and throws a fast ball across the plate. The batter hits a double off the center-field screen. Three men score. You scream: 'Send him to the showers!' The manager sends the pitcher off the field as the home crowd boos. How would you feel if you were the pitcher?

"Sometimes we say: 'Mr. M. is a terrible teacher. He can't keep order in the class. His lessons are dry as dust. If I were in charge, I wouldn't give exams. I wouldn't scold the kids if they came in late.' Imagine yourself in the place of your teacher. How would you handle the class?"

Rabbi Mayer continued. "Miriam says that her mother is very old-fashioned. She won't let her do things the other girls do. Miriam claims that she has a right to lead her own life. But her mother doesn't agree. Miriam is limited to dates on Saturday nights and holidays. She has to be in by midnight. She can't 'go steady' with her boy friend. Mother said 'no' when Miriam was invited to an out-of-town fraternity dance. Miriam feels that her mother is too strict, old-fashioned, and dictatorial. What if Miriam were in her mother's place?"

THINGS TO DISCUSS AND DO

1 Try to put yourself in the place of the following, and discuss in class:

a A Southern Negro enters a bus, and is asked by the driver to take a seat in the rear.

b A waitress in a busy restaurant is rushing to serve the customers. One man gets angry and says: "How long do I have to wait to be served here? Get going, girl, I'm in a hurry!"

c A high school teacher is unpopular with the students because he flunked the star athlete, making him ineligible for the big game.

d A girl whose parents were in a concentration camp in Germany is asked to room with a German exchange student who is visiting the United States for a year.

2 Select three incidents from the daily newspapers where the persons involved seem to be guilty. Show how further knowledge of the facts might change your opinion.

Some Other Sayings of the Fathers

Rabbi Mayer said: "If we listen we can hear the Still, Small Voice speaking to us through the wisdom of the *Pirke Aboth*. Let us consider some of the other 'Sayings.' For example, Rabbi Judah the Prince taught:

> *Be as careful in the case of a light precept as in that of a weighty one.*

Look up the meaning of 'precept'; explain what Rabbi Judah meant."

Tragedy in a Test Tube

A 28-year-old University of South Dakota medical researcher injected about two drops of a colorless liquid into the arms of two university employees, volunteers for a routine laboratory experiment. Twenty-four hours later, Jack Clifford and Mrs. Ardys Pearson were dead. A fatal mistake had been made.

Later in the week, the medical researcher told a coroner's jury that instead of picking up a vial of Demorol, he had picked up a vial of Methadon and administered 10 to 15 times more than he should have. He recognized his error five minutes later—but still too late. He told of the great care he had taken in the preparation of the vials and the measuring out of the synthetic, morphine-like drugs. But in the minor business of the routine injection, he had not been careful enough. Because of his carelessness, two people were dead. And his professional career came to an end.

"Sometimes," said Rabbi Mayer, "we look down upon commonplace rules of conduct and say to ourselves: 'These things aren't so important. I'll ignore them. When something important happens, then I'll make the right decision.'

"Rabbi Judah the Prince was trying to tell us to be just as careful in small matters as in important things. He believed that we can hear the Still, Small Voice in small matters, too.

Applying the Teaching of Rabbi Judah

"It seemed a small matter to Freddy when he copied the school assignment from his friend, even though the teacher had made a special point about each student doing his own work. However, Freddy would never think of telling a lie. When the teacher asked him if he had copied the assignment, Freddy admitted it. Later he said that copying someone else's work didn't seem like such a terrible thing, but that he would never tell a lie.

"How does Rabbi Judah's teaching apply to Freddy?"

The Rabbi went on. "Rosalind didn't like Linda. She told all her friends that Linda was stuck-up and a snob, and said other unkind things about the way Linda dressed and acted. However, when some of the girls planned a party and decided not to invite Linda, Rosalind said they were being unfair, that she wouldn't let them hurt Linda in that way. As a result, the girls invited Linda.

"How does Rabbi Judah's teaching apply to Rosalind?

The Scale of Merit

"Joshua ben Perachyah taught:

Judge every man by the scale of merit.

"Rabbi Joshua ben Perachya listened to the Still, Small Voice. He asks us to judge each person, of any religion, creed, or race, on the basis of merit. It is not easy to do this, yet it is one of the most important parts of the democratic way of life. Too many of us allow our prejudices to interfere with our judgment. All too often we judge by the scale of wealth, the scale of social position, the scale of religion, and the scale of neighborhood."

TEST YOURSELF

1 Do you choose your candidate in a school election on the scale of merit?

2 Do you feel that the janitor of the school or synagogue is your equal? Or do you consider him a servant, and therefore beneath you? Would you invite him to your home for dinner?

3 Do you show more respect to rich people than to poor ones?

4 Do you choose friends from poor neighborhoods just as easily as from rich ones?

5 Do you ever find yourself liking or disliking someone because he or she is a Protestant, a Catholic, or a Jew?

6 Do you believe that Americans are superior to Europeans?

7 If you had a teacher who was an educated American Indian, would you accept and judge him as you would any other teacher? Or would you feel there was something different and odd about him?

Three Crowns

"Rabbi Simeon said:

> *There are three crowns: the crown of Torah, the crown of the priesthood, and the crown of kingship. But the crown of a good name excels them all.*

"What do you think Rabbi Simeon meant?"

THINGS TO DISCUSS AND DO

1 Ecclesiastes taught: *A good name is better than precious oil.* The Rabbis explained this by saying:

Good oil evaporates and becomes less and less, but a good name becomes greater and greater; good oil is used only at times, but a good name lasts forever; good oil can be bought for money, but a good name comes unbought to all who deserve it; good oil can be used only by the living, but a good name endures even after death; good oil can be owned only by the rich, but a good name by rich and poor alike if they truly deserve it.

2 Names are very important to us. We react favorably or unfavorably to them because they remind us of something. Give your reactions to the following names and tell your first thoughts on hearing the name:

Napoleon Bonaparte	Louis Pasteur
Wilbur Wright	Thomas Jefferson
Jack Dempsey	Aaron Burr
Abraham Lincoln	Adolf Hitler
Haman	Jeremiah
Babe Ruth	Albert Einstein
Haym Salomon	Eleanor Roosevelt

3 How do you think people react when they hear your name? Do they associate it with character, honesty, truthfulness, troublemaking, laziness, selfishness, reliability, energy, meanness, kindness, uncooperativeness, helpfulness? People identify your name with *you!* Have you earned a good name or a bad one? Do you agree with Rabbi Simeon about the importance of a good name?

Judging by Appearances

"Rabbi Meir said:

> *Look not at the pitcher, but at that which is in it. There may be a new pitcher which is full of old wine, and an old pitcher which has not even new wine in it.*

"The Still, Small Voice asks us to refrain from judging by appearances, by the external things," declared Rabbi Mayer. "Judaism has never been particularly concerned with the physical appearance of its teachers and leaders, whether they were tall or short, heavy or thin, handsome or ugly. Judaism is interested in character, not looks; in the significance of the teaching and not the appearance of the teacher. We know little of the looks of Abraham, Moses, Isaiah, or Hillel. We know much of the wise and moral teachings of these God-inspired men.

"Moses Mendelssohn was a hunchback. Judged by his looks alone, little would have been thought of him. Yet he was one of the greatest philosophers of his age, a man of courageous spirit and profound intelligence. Moses Mendelssohn translated the entire Bible from Hebrew into German, a tremendous achievement.

"Napoleon Bonaparte was a little man. Yet he dominated the entire continent of Europe. He was not judged by his appearance, but rather by what he did for good and for evil.

"Many thought Abraham Lincoln the ugliest of men. Yet we do not judge him by his appearance. History will always remember his contributions to our democracy, the goodness of his character, and the real measure of his devotion to America.

"The Talmud tells us about Rabbi Eleazar, the son of Rabbi Simon, who was on his way to begin work in his new congregation. Riding on his donkey, his heart was filled with pride and haughtiness because of his learning. An ugly man of dwarfed appearance greeted him: 'Peace be unto you, rabbi.' Instead of returning his greeting with courtesy, the rabbi said: 'How ugly the man is! Tell me, are all the other men of your city as ugly as you?' The dwarf replied: 'I do not know. Go and tell the Divine Craftsman who made me: How ugly is this, the vessel Thou hast made.'

"Rabbi Eleazar was sorry for the way he had spoken. All the way to the village, he pleaded with the dwarf to forgive him. But the dwarf refused to listen to him. When they reached the village, the rabbi told the townspeople that he was unworthy to be their rabbi because of his pride and haughtiness. Moved by his tears, and impressed with his sincere repentance, the townspeople persuaded the dwarf to forgive him. Rabbi Eleazar was never filled with arrogance again. He had learned his lesson; never again would he judge from outer appearances."

JUDGING THE CONTENTS BY THE PACKAGE

1 To what extent do you judge by outer appearances?

2 Do you judge a book by its cover?

3 Have you ever judged a person by his or her looks, and found that you were mistaken? Give examples.

4 In choosing a husband or a wife, are good looks more important than character?

5 How important are appearances when a congregation selects a new Rabbi?

6 Which is more precious to a congregation—a brand-new Torah, or one which is very old and has been used by the congregation for many years?

7 A small child will usually choose the largest and most elaborate package during Hanukkah. It may contain a very inexpensive toy. The smallest package of all may contain a costly watch or ring. The child judges by outer appearances. The more mature person does not. It is a sign of childishness to judge from the outer covering. It is a sign of growing up to judge from the contents of the package itself.

How would you apply this to your judgment of people?

The Good Way

Continuing the discussion of the Sayings of the Fathers, Rabbi Mayer said, "Rabbi Judah the Prince once asked:

Go and see which is that good way to which a man should cleave.

"*In answer, Rabbi Eleazar said: 'A good eye.' Rabbi Joshua said: 'A good associate.' Rabbi Jose said: 'A good neighbor.' Rabbi Simeon said: 'One who sees the events.' Rabbi Elazar said: 'A good heart.' And Rabbi Judah said to them: 'I approve the words of Elazar ben Arach more than your words, for in his words yours are included.'*

"The real question was: What is the most important requirement of a good life; what is the clue to the right way of living? This is how the rabbis interpreted the answers: A good eye means freedom from envy. A good associate means friendship. A good neighbor means sympathy. One who sees the event is the ability to learn from our past deeds. A good heart means unselfish love in thought, feeling, and actions. And this last includes all the others."

Rabbi Mayer rose. "Sometimes people explain: 'I don't attend synagogue services; I don't observe Jewish ceremonies. I don't belong to Jewish organizations, and I don't believe in giving to charity. I don't know much about Judaism but—I am a Jew at heart!'

"Is such a person really a Jew at heart?

"Suppose someone said to you: 'I'm not interested in American history, literature, or culture. I never vote. I never contribute to the support of American institutions. I never observe American customs or traditions. I have never identified myself with the hopes and dreams of democracy but—I am an American at heart.'

"Is such a person really an American at heart?

"How does a Jew earn the right to say 'I am a Jew at heart'?

"How does an American earn the right to say: 'I am an American at heart'?

"Explain what you think Rabbi Elazar ben Arach really meant by 'a good heart.' "

QUESTIONS FOR DISCUSSION

1 What did Hillel mean when he said: *If I am not for myself, who will be for me? And when I am for myself alone, what am I? And if not now, when?*

2 What did Rabbi Tarphon mean when he said: *It is not entirely up to you to finsh the work, nor art thou free to desist from it.*

3 "For the sake of heaven" means a noble cause or worthy purpose. What is meant by this: "Every controversy that is for the sake of heaven will, in the end, be established. Every one which is not for the sake of heaven will not, in the end, be established."

Which of the following are controversies for the sake of heaven?

a Allan is attending a meeting of the Student Council. The discussion has been pleasant and harmonious. He knows that if he brings up the question of the rude and noisy behavior of the students during assembly periods, there will be a bitter and angry debate. But several guest speakers have been annoyed by the students' behavior. Should Allan remain silent?

b A teacher has talked about America as a Christian nation, and the high school as a Christian school. Some of the Bible readings in class have been followed by comments from the teacher that the "Jews crucified Jesus." Should the Jewish students do something about this? What course of action, if any, should be taken?

c Dorothy is angry because she wasn't elected School Secretary. It had been agreed that there would be no electioneering for any of the candidates. Dorothy's friends did not campaign for her. Her opponent's friends made telephone calls, wrote letters, and urged the students to vote for their candidate. Dorothy's supporters want her to make a fuss so that the school authorities will hold another election, and give her friends a chance to win support for her. Her father is a prominent businessman and a good friend of the Chairman of the Board of Education. What should Dorothy do?

d Melvin was late for school. He hitched a ride. The driver announced that America was going to the dogs. He said: "What we need is a dictator in this country," and insisted that the government deport all foreigners. He asked Melvin if he didn't agree. Melvin hated everything the man said. He wanted to tell him what he really thought—and yet, the man had been kind enough to pick him up. What would you have done?

4 Which *Sayings of the Fathers* apply to the following:
  a Hospitality.
  b Silence.
  c Your neighbor's property.
  d How to be honored by men.
  e A leopard, eagle, gazelle, and lion.
Look up the answers in *Sayings of the Fathers*, by Hertz. Which apply to a, b, c, d, and e?
  Ch. II:17; Ch. I:5; Ch. IV:8; Ch. I:17; Ch. V:23.

5 There are four characters of men described in the *Pirke Aboth*:
  He who says: *What is mine is mine, this is the average type.*
  He who says: *What is mine is thine, and what is thine is mine, is undisciplined.*
  He who says: *What is mine is thine, and what is thine is thine, is a saint.*
  He who says: *What is thine is mine, and what is mine is mine, is wicked.*
  Which character do you resemble?

6 Simeon the Just used to say: *Upon three things the world stands: upon Torah, upon worship, and upon the showing of kindness.* If Simeon the Just lived in an atomic age, how do you think he would explain the way Torah, Worship and Kindness could bring peace to our world?

7 In the *Pirke Aboth* we read: *Where there is no Torah, there are no manners: Where there are no manners, there is no Torah.* What do good manners have to do with Torah? How would you explain this?

8 Nittai the Arbelite said: *Be not doubtful of retribution.* Retribution means that you are punished for evil and rewarded for good. How are we rewarded and punished in this life? A person may cheat or lie and seem to get away with it. An individual may do a good deed and not receive any reward. Was Nittai correct in his promise of retribution?

9 How do you think the Sayings of the Fathers help us to solve the mystery of the Still, Small Voice?

SELECTED QUOTATIONS

The Pursuit of Peace

Hillel said, "Be of the disciples of Aaron, the High Priest, loving peace and pursuing it . . ."

How should one love peace; how should one pursue it? By bringing it about between one's immediate neighbors thus reconciling the small quarrels of the world ere they become greater ones.

And this was Aaron's wont. If he saw two men quarreling with one another, he would go and visit one and say to him, "My son, dost thou know what thy companion is doing at this moment? He is beating his breast and rending his garments saying, 'Woe unto me! How can I ever face my friend again? I am full of shame that I sinned against him and began this quarrel!'" He would address him in this vein until the hatred which this man bore against his companion became dissipated.

Aaron would then hurriedly run to the other participant in the quarrel and say to him, "My son, see what your friend saith now. He beats his breast, and tears his garments and repents of having quarreled with you." And Aaron would stay with the second quarreler until he, too, would regret his strife. Thereupon Aaron would arrange an apparently accidental meeting between the two men whose friendship was thus renewed.

It is for this reason that the children of Israel wept for Aaron for thirty days after his death.

ABOTH D' RABBI NATHAN, CH. 12

Pirke Aboth

On the long Sabbath afternoons of summer, it is customary to read in the synagogue a chapter of the Mishnah tractate popularly called "The Sayings of the Fathers (Pirke Aboth)." Dating back to Talmudic times and the academy of Sura, this custom established Aboth, or Fathers, in the Jewish consciousness like no other section of the Mishnah or, indeed, the Talmud. And the reason for this is not difficult to find. The 'Sayings of the Fathers' is in many ways a unique part of the Mishnah, that compilation of the oral tradition set down in its final form sometime near the end of the 2nd Century of the Common Era by Judah the Holy, usually known as Rabbi.

MICHAEL WYSCHOGROD

Who Is Mighty?

Samuel Ibn Nagrela was a Spanish-Jewish poet of the eleventh century, vizier to the King of Granada. One day he was cursed in the presence of the king, who commanded Samuel to punish the offender by cutting out his tongue. The Jewish vizier, however, treated his enemy kindly, whereupon the curses became blessings. When the king next noticed the offender, he was astonished that Samuel had not carried out his command. Samuel replied, "I have torn out his angry tongue, and given him instead a kind one." The rabbis rightly declared, "Who is mighty? He who makes his enemy his friend."

Wisdom and Deeds

Rabbi Eleazer ben Azaryah used to say, "One whose wisdom is greater than his deeds, what is he like? A tree whose branches are many and whose roots few, and the wind comes and roots it up and overturns it on its face. But one whose deeds exceed his wisdom, what is he like? A tree whose branches are few and its roots many, so that even if all the winds that are in the world come and blow upon it, they stir it not from its place."

Aboth III:22

The Humanity of Jewish Wisdom

In my early youth I read—I have forgotten where—the words of the ancient Jewish sage—Hillel, if I remember rightly: "If thou art not for thyself, who will be for thee? But if thou art for thyself alone, wherefore art thou?"

The inner meaning of these words impressed me with its profound wisdom, and I interpreted them for myself in this manner: I must actively take care of myself, that my life should be better, and I must not impose the care of myself on other people's shoulders; but if I am going to take care of myself alone, of nothing but my own personal life, it will be useless, ugly, meaningless. This thought ate its way deep into my soul, and I say now with conviction: Hillel's wisdom served as a strong staff on my road, which was neither even nor easy.

I believe that Jewish wisdom is more all-human and universal than any other; and this not only because of its immemorial age, not only because it is the first born, but also because of the powerful humaneness that saturates it, because of its high estimate of man.

MAXIM GORKY

Where There Is No Torah

Rabbi Eleazar, the son of Azaryah, said: "Where there is no Torah, there are no manners; where there are no manners, there is no Torah; where there is no wisdom, there is no reverence for God; where there is no reverence for God, there is no wisdom; where there is no knowledge, there is no understanding; where there is no understanding, there is no knowledge; where there is no meal, there is no Torah; where there is no Torah, there is no meal."

Aboth, III:21

The Test of a Cultured Person

There are seven marks of an uncultured, and seven of a wise, man.

The wise man does not speak before him who is greater than he in wisdom; and does not break in upon the speech of his fellow; he is not hasty to answer; he questions according to the subject matter, and answers to the point; he speaks upon the first thing first, and upon the last thing last; regarding that which he has not understood, he says, "I do not understand it," and he acknowledges the truth. The reverse of all this is to be found in an uncultured man.

Aboth, Chapter V:10

Strategy of Love

From the purely humanitarian standpoint, the most important saying in the first chapter (of Pirke Aboth) is that of Hillel, "Be thou a disciple of Aaron, loving peace and pursuing peace, loving all creatures and drawing them near to the Torah." Love is regarded as the due of all God's creatures, and it is more than likely that this noble saying envisages the hope, held in wide circles, of winning the world to Torah through the strategy of love.

Universal Jewish Encyclopedia

THINGS TO DO

1 Antigonos of Socho used to say: *Be not like servants who minister to their master upon the condition of receiving a reward; but be like servants who minister to their master without the condition of receiving a reward.*

Write an essay explaining this statement. In it tell of incidents in your life where you did something fine and good without any thought of recognition or reward.

2 List the professions that apply to Chapter II:1 of the *Sayings of the Fathers.*

3 Read the story of the Rebellion of Korach in the Bible (Numbers 16), and decide whether this was a controversy for the sake of heaven, or not.

4 Hillel used to say: *In a place where there are no men, strive to be a man.* Discuss this statement in class. Tell of situations where a boy or girl of your own age might apply the teachings of Judaism to prevent an injustice to another individual or another group.

5 Define and describe: Wisdom, Greatness, Wealth, and Fame. Then read the definitions of Ben Zoma in Chapter IV:1, of the *Pirke Aboth*. Select a nationally-known personality; using these definitions, write a character analysis of how wise, mighty, rich and honored you think that person really is.

6 Joshua ben Perachya taught: *Judge every man by the scale of merit*. Select statements from the Declaration of Independence and the Bill of Rights to show how the American way of life supports the teaching of this wise rabbi.

7 Read the complete *Sayings of the Fathers* and choose the most important verse. In class, justify your selection and tell how it helps you follow the commandments of the Still, Small Voice.

SUGGESTED READINGS

Feuer, Leon. *Jewish Literature Since the Bible*, I. Pp. 22–23.
Herford, R. Travers. *Pirke Aboth*.
Hertz, Joseph. *Sayings of the Fathers*.
Singer, S. *Authorized Daily Prayerbook*. Pp. 184–209.
Union Prayerbook. Pp. 165–178.
Universal Jewish Encyclopedia, Vol. I. Pp. 32–33.

9

THE VOICE OF THE RABBIS
The Ethics of the Talmud and Midrash

The Most Important Question of Life

"My Friend: I am asking you the most important question of your life. Your joy or your sorrow for all ETERNITY depends upon it. The question is: ARE YOU SAVED? It is not if you are a member of some church, but, are you SAVED? It is not how good you are, but, ARE YOU SAVED? No one can enjoy the blessings of God or go to Heaven without being saved. . . ."

The Pamphlet

This was the pamphlet that Melvin gave to the Rabbi as the class began. Rabbi Mayer looked at it and then read it aloud.

Turning to Melvin, he asked:

"Where did you find this?"

"I was sitting on the porch after school yesterday when a man came up and asked to see Mother. I told him she was downtown shopping. He started to leave, and then he came back to me and said: 'Sonny, are you saved? God won't love you unless you believe as I do.' I didn't understand him, so I said: 'What do you mean, am I saved? Why won't God love me?' Then he handed me the pamphlet and walked away."

"I'm glad you brought this pamphlet to class, Melvin. Let's talk about it for a while," said the Rabbi. "There are people who want everyone to believe exactly as they believe. I'm sure you recall the story of Sodom and Gomorroh, and why God was angry with their inhabitants. Sandra, do you remember?"

"I think it had something to do with the legend about a bed, and strangers who were made to fit the exact size of the bed. The story meant that everybody had to be the same and think the same."

"Yes, Sandra," said Rabbi Mayer. "And the man who gave the pamphlet to Melvin is just like that. He insists that everyone believe as he believes. Then they will be 'saved,' and will go to heaven when they die. If they disagree, God will not love them, and may even punish them."

"But that doesn't sound right. That isn't so," retorted Judy indignantly. "Everybody has the right to worship God in his own way."

"That is true," the Rabbi agreed. "In this blessed land of freedom the Christian worships in his church, and the Jew worships in his synagogue or temple. Each respects the beliefs and the convictions of the other."

"But that man said God only loves those who believe a certain way. Do you think that could be so?" questioned Melvin.

"No, Melvin," answered Rabbi Mayer. "Both Judaism and Christianity teach that every person is precious in the sight of God, and that He loves us all as His children. The United States Constitution guarantees freedom of religion, the right of each individual to worship God as he chooses. Brothers and sisters don't always agree, or have the same ideas or beliefs, but their father loves each of them. So it is with our Heavenly Father."

God's Love for All

"Does the Bible teach this?" asked Martin.

"Yes, it does. The Bible says that man is created in the image of God. It doesn't say anything about his color or his religion or what any one man believes. Do you remember the Book of Amos? What did God say to the children of Israel when they began to think that God loved them more than the others?"

Sylvia raised her hand. "I remember. It impressed me so much when I read it. God said:

> *Are ye not as the children of the Ethiopians unto Me, O children of Israel?*

"This meant that God loved the dark-skinned Ethiopians as His children, too."

"That is correct, Sylvia. And what did the prophet Malachi teach?"

Harold waved his hand. The Rabbi nodded to him and he said:

> *Have we not all one Father, hath not one God created us?*

Bernard asked again: "Does it say this anywhere else? I mean, is it only in the Bible?"

The Talmud and Midrash

"The Bible is only one part of Jewish literature," said the Rabbi. "It is a very important part, and a very sacred part, but there is much more. There are great and wise teachings in the Talmud and the Midrash. In these works we read of the teachers and sages who

studied the Bible very carefully and explained what the Bible really
meant. We hear the voices of these learned rabbis and sages speaking to us through the pages of the Talmud and Midrash."

"I'm going to ask you to look up some facts about the Talmud
and Midrash for your next assignment. But first I want you to listen
to what this remarkable literature has to say about the equality of
man, and God's love for all His children.

Out of the Dust

"The Talmud teaches the equality of men. One of the rabbis
said that when God decided to create man out of dust, He caused
the winds to blow, and the dust from the four corners of the earth
gathered in one spot. It was out of this dust that man was created,
in order that the people of one country should not say: 'The first
man was created out of the dust of our land,'—and another country
should not say: 'the first man was created out of the dust of our
soil.' The dust came from everywhere; hence all peoples have the
same beginning.

"The rabbis also tell us that the law was given on Mount Sinai
in seventy voices, corresponding to the seventy languages of the
time. Thus the Ten Commandments were given to all peoples. They
were not given in any one king's land, not in any city or inhabited
spot, but in the desert, a vast space that does not belong to any
land or any people, but belongs to God.

The Greatest Principle of Judaism

"In the second century, Rabbi Akiba, son of Joseph, was asked
about the greatest principle of Judaism. He said it was the commandment in Leviticus:

Thou shalt love thy neighbor as thyself.

When God said 'neighbor,' He did not say anything about the
neighbor's religion, or the color of his skin.

"His friend, Rabbi Simeon, son of Azzai, disagreed. He said the greatest verse is from Genesis:

> *This is the book of the generations of man. In the day that God created man, in the likeness of God made He him.*

Notice that it says 'This is the book of the generations of *Man*.' God's word is meant for all people, not for the Jews alone. You can see why Rabbi Simeon thought this so important. The Still, Small Voice taught him that man is created in the image of God, that all people are the children of God."

For Jews Only?

Gilbert raised his hand, and when the Rabbi called on him he said: "The other day we had a discussion after school, walking home with some of our Christian friends. One boy asked us why Jews thought they were better than others. Another fellow wanted to know why we thought that God didn't love any people but the Jews. That didn't sound right to me, but I didn't know what to answer."

"Many Jews can't answer questions about their own faith, Gil," said the Rabbi. "That is why a good Jewish education is so important. There are people who think that the Jewish religion is only interested in the welfare of Jews. You will hear it said that we are narrow and clannish, that as a Chosen People we believe God loves us above all others. This is not true.

"The Talmud not only says that God loves those of every religious faith, but it also teaches that no matter what kind of work a man may do to earn an honest livelihood, his efforts are pleasing to God."

The Rabbi walked to the bookshelf and took down a volume. It looked very large, and very old. He leafed through the pages, and then he read:

"I am the creature of God and so is my fellow-man; my calling is in the town, and his in the fields; I go early to my work, and he to his; he does not boast of his labor nor I of mine, and if thou shouldst say, 'I accomplish great things and he little things,' we have learned that whether a man accomplish great things or small, his reward is the same if only his heart be set upon Heaven."

Rabbi Mayer paused in his reading and looked at the class. "Does this statement from the Talmud sound narrow? As we study Rabbinic literature, the Talmud and the Midrash, we are taught that 'sometimes the mortal father prefers one child to another, but He that created the world extends His love to all His children. His tender mercies are over all His works.'

The Talmudic Method

"The concept of God's love for all is developed magnificently in the interpretation of the verse, Leviticus 18:5:

> *Ye shall therefore keep My statutes and Mine ordinances which if a man do he shall live by them.*

Now listen carefully, and you will see how the rabbis analyzed the Bible and found in it new and more wonderful meanings. This is the famous Talmudic method of teaching.

"The rabbis ask: 'How do we know that a Gentile who obeys the Torah is the equal of the High Priest? From the words of the verse: "which if a man do he shall live by them."' Notice that it does not say Jew or Gentile, but *man*—meaning any man of any faith.

"It is also said: *This is the law of mankind* (II Samuel 7:19). It is *not* said, This is the law of the priests, or the Levites, or of Israel, but

> *This is the law of mankind.*

"The Book of Isaiah says (26:2):

> *Open the gates that the righteous Gentile or nation that*
> *keepeth faithfulness may enter in.*

It does *not* say: Open the gates that the priests or Levites or Israel-ites may enter. The righteous of every faith and every nation have their share in God's love.

"In the days of the Temple, when sacrifices were offered to God, they were offered for all humanity. God is not the Father of the Jews alone, but the Heavenly Father of all. God is not only the King of Israel; He is the King of the Universe. This is what the rabbis taught the Jewish people about the universal God."

I Call Heaven and Earth

Rabbi Mayer's voice was gentle, and the class could see how deeply these teachings of the Talmud moved him. As the clock neared the end of the hour, he said: "I want you to remember this teaching of the rabbis:

> *I call heaven and earth to witness that whether it be Jew*
> *or non-Jew, man or woman, free or bondsman—only ac-*
> *cording to their acts does the Divine Spirit rest upon them.*

"The Still, Small Voice, speaking through the Talmud and Mid-rash does not say that any one people or faith has a monopoly on God's love. It does not say that we have to believe a certain way to be saved. Only according to our deeds, only according to our acts, do we earn the blessing of God's love."

WHAT DO YOU THINK?

1 How do you feel about the tract, "The Most Important Question of Life"?

2 What answer would you have given the man who said to Melvin: "Are you saved?"

3 Do you think the average Christian is interested in converting Jews to Christianity?

4 Do you think Judaism should have missionary organizations to convert Christians to Judaism?

5 Are Jews as concerned as Christians about punishment and reward in the next world? Why?

6 It has been said that "Judaism is a religion of deed and not creed." What does this statement mean?

7 Do you think God loves His children even when they do wrong?

8 How should the Talmudic teaching that all people are God's children influence us in our relationships with those of other races and religions?

A Great Ocean of Learning

When the class met again, Rabbi Mayer began the session by saying: "I don't expect you to become learned Talmudic scholars in this short time. Some men give a lifetime to the study of the Talmud, and even then they are able to take but 'one drop out of the great ocean of learning.' But I do hope that as we study the wisdom of the rabbis, we will gain a greater appreciation of Judaism as a way of life. We will learn to apply Judaism in our own everyday relationships with others. We will put Judaism to work. Perhaps then we may solve the mystery of the Still, Small Voice."

And Doing

Rabbi Mayer continued: "The rabbis did not think of religion as prayer, or ritual, or learning, alone. Everything a person does, at home, at work, at play, is a part of Judaism too. That is why the Talmud not only contains teachings about God, the sacredness of man, the importance of prayer, the lessons of the Torah, but also considers every aspect of life. A Table of Contents for the Talmud would include problems of marriage and divorce, the education of children, respect for parents, duties of the workman and the employer, the obligation to help the poor, and the importance of honesty, truthfulness, and kindness in our dealings with others. Even the care of the body and rules for good health are part of the religious life.

"The God of justice demands justice from those who worship Him. Therefore the rabbis gave a great deal of thought to criminal law—judges and witnesses, fair trials, and merciful verdicts. But there is more to law than the hearing of criminal cases. The rabbis pondered over civil law, quarrels and lawsuits over property, damages, inheritance rights, and the buying and selling of merchandise. Almost anything you can think of can be found in the Talmud: education, medicine, astronomy, law—even juggling!"

"Juggling?" the class echoed almost as one voice.

"Yes, juggling," said the Rabbi. "All of us have marveled at the amazing balance and coordination of jugglers. But I wonder how many of those we have seen could match the skill of Rabbi Simeon ben Gamaliel.

"According to the Talmud, at one holiday feast he amazed everyone by juggling eight burning torches. We are told that he could reach over and kiss the ground without bending his body.

"The Talmud tells us about another juggler who used open knives, keeping seven of them in the air at the same time. Still another juggler used eggs and astounded his audience with his skill.

Rip van Winkle of the Talmud

"You all know the legend of Rip van Winkle, I'm sure," said Rabbi Mayer. "Let me tell you the story of Choni, the Rip van Winkle of the Talmud:

One day, while walking along the road, Choni saw a man planting a carob tree, and said to him, "Since a carob tree does not bear fruit for seventy years, how can you be certain of living long enough to eat from it?" The man answered: "I found the world filled with carob trees; as my forefather planted them for me, I likewise plant them for my descendants." Choni thereupon sat down, had his meal and fell asleep. While he slumbered, a grotto grew around him so that he was hidden from view. And he slept for seventy years.

On awakening, he saw a man gathering carobs from the very carob tree. Choni asked him, "Do you know who planted this carob tree?" The reply came: "My grandfather." Choni exclaimed, "Surely seventy years have passed like a dream!"

Then he went to his house and inquired whether the son of Choni the Circle-drawer still lived. They told him that his son was no more, but his grandson was living. He said to them, "I am Choni," but they would not believe him. He went to the Academy where he heard the rabbis say, "Our studies are now as clear as in the time of Choni the Circle-drawer; for when he entered the Academy he used to solve all the difficulties of the scholars." He said to them, "I am Choni," but they would not believe him or pay him the honor due to him. He thereupon prayed to God that he might die, and he died. Hence arose the proverb, "Either companionship or death."

"Through the Talmud, the Still, Small Voice teaches us loyalty and devotion to our friends. It tells us to join with them to prepare for the future. It warns against laziness and selfishness. It emphasizes honest work and diligent effort at all times, so that we should not waste our years on earth."

The Dignity of Honest Labor

After the Rabbi finished the story, Lillian said: "I never thought that a holy book like the Talmud would have stories about jugglers and a Rip van Winkle. It seems—well, it seems sort of funny. Just think of a rabbi who juggles. I always thought of a rabbi as a scholar and a teacher, a man who is above things like that. It just doesn't seem dignified to tell such stories about rabbis."

Rabbi Mayer laughed and said: "All right. I'll tell you about some other rabbis who didn't spend all of their time studying and teaching. They were too busy working in order to buy food for themselves and their families. They believed that any honest work was dignified. In those days rabbis didn't receive salaries from the congregation or the community. Rabbi Akiba collected bundles of wood and sold them. Rabbi Joshua was a charcoal-burner. Rabbi Meir was a scribe. Rabbi Jose ben Chalaphta was a worker in leather, Rabbi Jochanan made sandals, Rabbi Judah was a baker, and Rabbi Abba Saul was a kneader of dough. It was because they labored, too, that they were firmly convinced of the dignity of honest labor. They heard the Still, Small Voice through their work. These same rabbis told the following legend:

At the time the Holy One, Blessed be He, informed Adam, "Thorns and thistles shall the earth bring forth to thee" (Gen. 3:18), his eyes filled up with tears. Adam said to God, "Sovereign of the Universe, am I and my donkey to feed in the same manger?" But, when God added, "In the sweat of thy brow shalt thou eat bread," he immediately became calm. The moral is that through his labor, man raises himself above the rest of the animal kingdom.

Religion at Work

"The rabbis, obedient to the Still, Small Voice, insisted upon justice for the laboring man. The employer must be considerate toward the men working for him. He must protect their rights at all times, and be thoughtful and kind even when the law does not specifically compel him to be so. The following story illustrates the point:

The porters engaged by Rabba bar Bar Chanah broke a cask of wine belonging to him, and as a penalty he took their coats from them. They went to Rab and complained, and Rab ordered Rabba to restore the garments. He asked, "Is that the law?" Rab replied, "It is, for it is written, 'That thou mayest walk in the way of good men' (Prov. 2:20). He gave them back their coats. The laborers then said: "We are poor and have toiled throughout the day and are hungry; we are in great need." Rab said to Rabba, "Go and pay their wages." He asked, "Is that the law?" He replied, "Yes, for it is written, 'And keep the paths of the righteous.' " (Prov. 2:20).

"The Talmud did not forget the rights of the employer. The rabbis taught that a workman must be faithful in his work, and not cheat his employer in any way. He must give his employer his best efforts.

It is told of Abba Joseph the builder that his opinion was sought on a certain matter, and he was found standing upon some scaffolding. The questioner said to him, "I want to ask you something"; but his answer was, "I cannot come down because I am hired by the day."

"Abba Joseph felt that he had no right to use any of the time for which his employer paid him to solve the problems of others. A similar story is told about Abba Hilkiah, the grandson of Choni the circle-drawer:

Two scholars went to him to ask that he should pray for rain. They did not find him at his house. They proceeded to the field and found him ploughing the ground. They greeted him cordially, but he took no notice of them, and never halted his ploughing. When he returned home he found the two rabbis waiting for him. They asked him why he had ignored their greeting. He replied: "I hired myself out for the day, and I was of the opinion that I had no right to interrupt my work and thus cheat my employer."

"The rabbis of the Talmud worked with the people and under-stood their problems. When they taught the people, they spoke in words the people could understand. That is why there are so many stories. The people loved to learn the lessons of Judaism through these stories, stories of the commonplace things of life, stories about trees, the oil of olives, sand, water, the sun, moon and stars. Every story had a purpose: to teach important and inspir-ing lessons about Judaism as a way of life, and to help people solve the mystery of the Still, Small Voice.

Israel and an Olive

"The rabbis taught that Israel can be compared to an olive for three reasons. The first is this. In order for an olive to yield its essence, its best part, its oil, it must be subjected to pressure and crushed. So it is with the Jewish people. Whenever Israel has been subjected to pressure, and evil rulers have attempted to crush it, instead of giving up and surrendering to their will, the Jews made great contributions—not only to religious thinking, but to the arts and sciences as well.

"It is one of the wonders of history," said Rabbi Mayer, "that Israel has grown at times of persecution and pressure. The genius of the Bible, the wisdom of the Talmud, the brilliance of Jewish philosophy, the exalted hopes and dreams of Jewish poetry, did not flourish only at times of prosperity and peace, but during periods of persecution and misery. Many other peoples succumbed under pressure, but not the people of Israel. Each time their tormentors tried to destroy them, the best that was in them was called forth.

Courage in the Ghetto

"A remarkable document was discovered in Warsaw, Poland, by the Jewish Joint Distribution Committee. It tells of a scientific study of starvation, undertaken in the Warsaw Ghetto during World War II by a group of Jewish physicians and their families who were slowly and systematically starved to death by their Nazi jailers.

"The work began in February 1942. These 22 Jewish doctors knew that they were going to starve to death. Instead of merely crying against their fate, they added to human knowledge by making a precise technical study of the effects of starvation on the human mind and body. They had no instruments; they made their own. Remember: they were investigating the effects of starvation on themselves! The last remaining doctor smuggled out the reports and documents and had them buried, hoping that someday they would be found and would contribute to the growth of scientific knowledge.

"Couldn't these men have said: 'What's the use? Why contribute to a civilization that allows us to starve to death?' But even in the misery of the Warsaw Ghetto, even as their bodies weakened, they worked for science and humanity. They heard the Still, Small Voice."

The classroom was silent. This story of martyrdom and heroism was not just a lesson. It was something more than a story. This was the spirit of Judaism. This was the Israel the rabbis likened to an olive. Under pressure, even when crushed, there was the summons to give their best.

The Second Reason

"The second reason why Israel is compared to an olive," continued Rabbi Mayer, "is this. Take the oil of an olive and put it in an ordinary glass of water. Then see what happens when you try to mix it. Well, suppose you tell me what happens."

Leah said, "I think I know. You can't mix oil with water. The oil just won't mix."

"That is correct, Leah. Oil won't mix with water. It remains separate and apart. The rabbis in the Talmud explain to us that Israel must be like this. No, not that the Jewish people should not mix with their neighbors, but rather that the Jewish people must not mix with evil and become a part of tyranny and unrighteousness. Jews must be different, not in language or clothes, but in an ethical and moral way. Jews must never join with those who break God's laws of truth, righteousness and decency.

"Think about our history for a few moments. At a time when others worshipped idols, the Jews were different. They worshipped the One God.

"When some of their neighbors in biblical days sacrificed their first-born sons to the god Moloch, the Jews refused to follow this terrible custom. They were different. They listened to the Still, Small Voice.

"When they were urged to forget the laws of purity and decency, they remembered that they were 'a kingdom of priests and a holy people.' They had to be different. They heard the Still, Small Voice. They could not join in breaking the ethical commandments of their God.

"This doesn't mean that the Jews were perfect. Sometimes Jews forgot about their God and the moral precepts of Judaism; some Jews brought shame to their fellow-Jews. But as a people, most Jews have tried to stay away from cruel practices, dishonest dealings, and mob action against the weak and helpless."

As the Rabbi spoke, Lillian thought about the article she had clipped from the morning paper. She opened her purse and took it out. This is what she read:

NEGROES QUIT HOME AS NEIGHBORS PROTEST

PHILADELPHIA—(AP)—Their new home menaced for the second successive night by a street crowd muttering and shouting threats, a Negro family who moved into the house the past week decided against sleeping there Friday night.

About 8 P.M., Wiley J. Clarke and his wife, Blanche, about 26, entered a police car and were driven to the home of friends where they were guests overnight.

The Clarke house, bought in June for $6,500, is about two miles north of the city hall in an area where no other Negro families reside for several blocks.

When the Clarkes left Friday night, police estimated 300 persons were crowded outside the two-story row home. Occasionally, there were shouts, "why don't you get out of here?" and "get out of our neighborhood."

There was no serious disorder Friday night, in contrast to

Thursday when bricks and stones were hurled through several windows of the house.

Police estimated the crowd had grown to about 800 persons by midnight, and 300 were still there when police ordered the spectators to disperse at 2:30 A.M.

Lillian wondered: Were Jews members of the mob, shouting threats and throwing stones at the windows? Were Jews denying a family the right to live in its own home? Did Jews hate some of God's children because of the color of their skin? She hoped not, and uttered a silent prayer that modern Jews, too, would be like oil and refuse to mix with mob hatred, with cruelty, and prejudice.

The Third Reason

"Israel is compared to an olive for yet another reason. In my opinion," said Rabbi Mayer, "this is the most magnificent reason of all. If you take the oil of an olive and put it in a glass of water, what happens to it?"

Daniel answered quickly, "It rises to the top."

"That is right, Danny. No matter how you try to keep the oil at the bottom of the glass, in a very short time it rises to the top. How did the rabbis of the Talmud interpret this and apply it to Israel? Gilbert, what do you think?"

"I think it means that Jews should always try to rise to the top in their business or profession, just like oil always rises."

The Rabbi said: "Gil, you gave a reasonable answer. Jews should try to rise to the top in their business or professions. Whatever we do, we must always try our best to succeed. But I don't think that is the answer the rabbis would give. Judy, what do you think?"

Judy paused a moment before speaking. "It's a little hard to put into words, but it seems to me that the other two reasons had to do with—well, with great ideals, and, oh, I just can't find the right words."

"Take your time, Judy. You may be on the right track. Just think out loud."

Judy tried again. "When Abraham lifted his eyes to the mountain top, it meant to God. I remember the psalm: 'I will lift mine eyes.' Could it be that Israel should always try to lift itself upward on high to God?"

"I'm glad that you didn't give up, Judy, because that's exactly what the rabbis taught. That was the third reason. In every age, whenever tyrants insisted that the people of Israel give up their worship of God, Israel refused to listen. Whenever others tried to tempt the Jewish people to follow evil ways and ugly customs, Israel remembered the commandments of God. Israel heard the Still, Small Voice saying 'No.' Despite what others did, Israel tried to rise above hatred, cruelty and despair, toward the ways ordained by God. The Jews set their sights on high, that they might be worthy of being called a kingdom of priests and a holy people. They tried to remember the teaching of the Talmud: 'Israel is compared to an olive.' Just as oil rises to the top, so the Jew must always ascend on high to his God.

Man, the Child of God

"Today, we must still rise higher and higher in our efforts to find God and use God in our lives. Certainly we must rise above the thought that God is the God of one particular people, or that He only loves those of a certain faith. We must rise above the idea that we have to believe a certain way in order to be 'saved.'

"Judaism does not believe these things. Judaism does not say that you have to follow the Jewish religion in order to be saved. We believe in the teaching of the Talmud: that the righteous among all peoples and all religions have a share in the world to come. This means that everyone must try to live up to the highest ideals of his own faith. This means that we are all God's children, and that if we obey His commandments, we all have a share in

God's love. The Still, Small Voice speaks to us in many different languages, and through many different religious faiths."

Applying the Talmud

Rabbi Mayer looked at his watch. "We have just a few minutes more, and I haven't even begun to discuss some of the other important lessons of the Talmud. Actually, we haven't even taken a drop out of that great ocean of knowledge and wisdom—but I think that we are beginning to get an idea of how fascinating the study of the Talmud can be. We learned that the Still, Small Voice speaks of God's love for all His children. Now I want to give you an opportunity to think through your own interpretation of other *midrashim*, and stories of the Talmud."

WHAT THE TALMUD MEANS TO YOU

Seeing God

The Emperor said to Rabbi Joshua, son of Chananya: "I want to see your God." The Rabbi replied: "That is impossible." The Emperor said: "You must show Him to me, or I will punish you and your people." The Rabbi asked the Emperor to go outside with him. It was summer, and he said to the Emperor: "Look at the sun." He tried to look at the sun but it was too bright. "I cannot," said the Emperor. Then the Rabbi replied: "If you cannot even look at the sun, which is but one of the servants of the Holy One, Blessed be He, how shall you look at the Holy One Himself?"

The Talmud (*Chulin*)

How would you apply this to your belief in God?

The Power of God

One day a philosopher said to Rabbi Gamaliel: "If your God is so powerful, why doesn't He destroy the idols?" To which Gamaliel replied: "If the pagans worshipped those things the world did not need, God would surely destroy them. But see, they worship the sun, the moon, the stars, the planets, the springs, and the valleys. Shall He, because of these fools, destroy all of His beautiful universe?"

The Talmud

How would you apply this to the idols we worship today?

The Mercy of God

By something which he did, Rabbi brought upon himself the tribulations of sickness, and by something which he did, he rid himself of the sickness.

One day, as a calf was being led to the slaughterhouse, it fled toward the Rabbi, hid its head under his mantle, and wept. And Rabbi said: "Go, you were born for the slaughterhouse." Because he showed no pity to the beast, his sickness came upon him.

Another day, the servant of the Rabbi was sweeping the house. The cat and her kittens lay on the floor, and he would have swept them out, but Rabbi said to him: "Let them be, for it is written: 'The compassion of God is given to all His creatures.' " Because he pitied them, God pitied him, and he was cured.

The Talmud (Baba Mezia)

What does this story teach us about God? Is such a commonplace thing as kindness to animals a requirement of the Jewish faith?

Justice and Mercy

How does God balance His Justice and His Mercy? It may be likened to a king who had empty vessels. The king said, "If I put hot water into them, they will crack; if I put cold water into them, they will contract." What did the king do? He mixed the hot with the cold, and poured the mixture into the vessels, and they endured. Similarly said the Holy One, Blessed be He, "If I create the world only with the attribute of mercy, sins will multiply beyond all bounds; if I create it only with the attribute of justice, how can the world last! Behold, I will create it with both attributes; would that it might endure!"

Midrash Rabbah

Which quality do you think is more needed in the world: justice or mercy? Why?

Give examples where you can and should mix justice with mercy.

This Is Your Life

When Rome forbade Israel to teach the Torah, what did Akiba do? He called together great assemblies, and taught the Torah. Pappus, the son of Judah, came to him and said, "Akiba, do you not fear the Romans?" And Akiba replied: "Pappus, are you he whom they call wise? You are but a fool. I will relate a parable to you.

"A fox walked by the side of a stream, and in the water saw the fish scurrying about. 'Why do you flee?' he asked them. They replied: 'To escape from the nets which are spread for us.' And the fox said: 'Come out upon the land, and we will live together, as your fathers and my fathers lived together.' They replied: 'Are you indeed he whom they call the most cunning of animals? You are but a fool. If we are afraid here in the water, which is the place of our life, shall we not be all the more afraid on the land, which is the place of our death?'

"It is thus with us, Pappus," went on Akiba. "If we are afraid while we study the Torah, of which it is written: 'It is thy life, and the increase of Thy days,' shall we not be the more afraid if we cease from studying it?"

The Talmud (*Berochoth*)

How would you apply this tale to those who try to run away from the study and practice of Judaism?

The Golden Rule

A heathen once came to Shammai and said: "I will become a Jew on one condition; that you teach me the Law while I stand on one foot." Shammai took a stave and drove the mocker away. He then went to Hillel and said the same. "My son," said Hillel, "do not to your neighbor what you do not wish him to do to you. This is the law; all the rest is commentary."

The Talmud (Sabbath)

Is Hillel's statement an adequate explanation of Judaism?

Do you think that it is practical today to follow his teaching?

Describe three situations where it would be difficult to observe Hillel's rule.

Object Lesson

A woodsman went into the forest to ask the trees to give him wood for an axe. It seemed so modest a request that the principal trees at once agreed to it, and it was settled among them that the plain, homely ash should furnish what was wanted.

No sooner had the woodsman fitted the staff to his purpose than he began laying about him on all sides, felling the noblest trees in the forest. The oak whispered to the cedar, "Our first concession has lost us all. If we had not sacrificed our humblest neighbor, we ourselves might yet have stood for ages."

How would you interpret this Midrash?

How would you apply this to your relationship with your fellow-students?

Give an example of where a nation sacrificed a smaller nation, and then was destroyed or conquered itself.

The Evidence of Their Eyes

In commenting on the verse, "And the Lord came down to see the city and the tower (of Babel)" the Midrash remarks, "But did He need to come down? Are not all things known and revealed before the Almighty?" To which the answer is given, "God did this to teach mankind never to pass sentence, yea, not even to utter a single word on the basis of hearsay, but first to secure the evidence of their eyes."

The Midrash

Apply this Midrash to a situation where you accepted gossip instead of the facts—and the gossip was proven wrong.

What does this Midrash tell us about rumor and speculation?

The Guardians of the City

Rabbi Judah the Prince asked Rabbi Dosa and Rabbi Ammi to go forth and inspect the cities in the land of Israel.

They came to a city and said to the people, "Have the keepers of the city brought before us."

They brought the overseers.

Then they said to them: "Are these the keepers of the city?"

The people then brought forth the generals, the rich men, and the strongest of the city, but the rabbis asked: "Are these the keepers of the city?"

Then the people asked the rabbis: "Who then are the keepers of the city?"

The rabbis answered: "The teachers of the Scriptures and the tradition, who keep watch by day and by night, in accordance with the words: 'This book of the law shall not depart out of thy mouth, but thou shalt meditate therein day and night.'"

The Midrash

Why were the teachers the true guardians of the city?

Alexander and the Skull

Alexander the Great once came to a strange river. He followed it until he arrived at the gates of Paradise. There he lifted up his voice and cried out: "Open the door!" But a voice answered him: "These are the gates of the Eternal. None but the just shall pass."

"I am a great king," said Alexander. "Give me something to take away with me." A skull was thrown to him. He took the skull and placed it in one cup of a scale, and placed all his gold and silver in the other cup; but the skull still weighed it down.

He then asked the rabbis: "What does this mean?" They answered: "It is the eye of the skull, the eye of flesh and blood, which sees gold and silver and is never satisfied." Alexander asked: "How shall I know that what you say is true?" They answered: "Take a few grains of dust and cover the eye, and the cup of balance will rise, for it is written, 'the eye of man is never satisfied.'" Alexander put some dust in the eye, and the cup of the balance did rise. It no longer outweighed the cup with all the gold and silver.

The Talmud (Tamid)

What were the rabbis trying to tell Alexander? What can this story teach us?

The Lost Bracelet

When Rabbi Samuel visited Rome, he found a bracelet. The empress announced that she had lost a precious bracelet and offered a huge reward if it were returned in 30 days. Should the finder fail to return it in this time, he would forfeit his head.

Rabbi Samuel waited until the 30 days had passed before he returned the bracelet. He then admitted to the empress that he knew of her promise and her threat.

In reply to the perplexed look on her face, the wise old rabbi told her: "You must know that ethical Jewish conduct is inspired neither by hope of reward nor fear of punishment. It stems solely from the love of God, and the desire to do His commandments."

How can you apply this teaching to your life?

QUESTIONS FOR DISCUSSION

1   In the New Testament, Paul answers the question: "What must I do to be saved?" by saying "Believe in Jesus as the Lord and thou shalt be saved." What is Judaism's answer? How would you apply Psalm 15 to this question?

2   The Talmud records that for two and a half years the School of Shammai and the School of Hillel debated the question: "Would it have been better if man had never been created?" The disciples of Shammai said it would have been better if man had never been created. The disciples of Hillel disagreed. What is your opinion?

3   The rabbis argued as to whether we are God's children. Commenting on the text, "Ye are children of the Lord your God," Rabbi Judah said: "At the time that you conduct yourselves as dutiful children, you are called God's children; but when you do not so conduct yourselves, you are not called God's children." Rabbi Meir, on the other hand, declared that in either case the name of "God's children" applied, and insisted that even when we are unworthy we are still called "children of God." What do you think?

4   How would you apply the story of Choni the Circle-drawer to yourself and your classmates?

5   The Talmud uses the word *tzedakah*, or justice, for what we call charity. What do you think of the following quotation: "He that feeds the hungry feeds himself also, for charity blesses him that gives even more than him that takes"?

6   The Talmud attributes great importance to the role of the woman in determining the happiness of the home. A passage in the Talmud tells of a pious man who was married to a pious woman. Because they were childless, they divorced one another. The good man married a wicked woman, and she made him wicked. The good woman married a wicked man and she made him righteous. "It follows that all depends upon the woman." What are your reasons for agreeing or disagreeing with that statement?

7   Do you think that women would be able to serve as rabbis? Should a girl be admitted to rabbinical seminaries to prepare herself for the rabbinate? What would be the advantages and disadvantages of a woman rabbi?

8   At a Jewish Youth Council Institute held at Camp Le Foret, Colorado, dating between Jewish and non-Jewish youngsters was frowned upon as a step toward intermarriage. Is inter-dating harmful

or dangerous? If a Jewish boy or girl refuses to date someone of another faith, does this create ill will toward Jews? If we are all God's children, why object to mixed dating?

9 According to the Talmud, two witnesses are required to prove a case involving criminal law. Circumstantial evidence, however convincing, is not acceptable. A witness is allowed to testify only if he actually saw the crime. The Talmud tells of the following case: "We saw the accused run after a man with a sword in his hand. The man who was pursued entered a shop, and the accused entered the shop after him. There we saw the man was dead, and the sword, dripping with blood, was in the hand of the murderer." The testimony of these witnesses was not accepted because they had not seen the actual commission of the crime. What do you think of this Talmudic principle of law?

10 Talmud Sanhedrin states: "He who saves a life, it is as if he had saved the world; and he who destroys a life, it is as if he had destroyed the world." What does this mean to you? What does this tell us about the sanctity of the human personality?

11 When Rabbi Jochanan ben Zaccai was sick, his pupils came to visit him. When they saw him, they wept and said: "Rabbi, bless us." He replied: "May it please the Lord that you fear God as you fear men." His pupils were amazed, and asked: "Shall we not fear God more?" He replied: "May it please God that you fear Him as much. When a man commits a wrong, does he not say: 'If only no man has seen me.'" What do you think of this statement? Judging by your actions, do you fear man more than God?

THINGS TO DO

1 Look up the following in the Universal Jewish Encyclopedia, and write a paragraph explaining each:

Mishnah	Baraita	Halachah
Gemarah	Tannaim	Haggadah
Midrash	Amoraim	

2 Ask your rabbi to bring a copy of the Talmud to class, and to explain how the Mishnah and commentaries are used.

3 Write to the Hebrew Union College-Jewish Institute of Religion in Cincinnati, Ohio, and the Jewish Theological Seminary in New York, and ask about the necessary qualifications for entering the Rabbinate. Then read the chapter "The Rabbinical Student" in the book, *Students, Scholars and Saints*, by Louis Ginzberg. Compare the qualifications of the rabbinical student of yesterday and today.

4 Debate the proposition, Resolved: Women can serve in the Rabbinate just as capably and effectively as men.

5 Read the story of Rip van Winkle in *The Sketch Book* of Washington Irving, and write an essay comparing it with the story of Choni, the Jewish Rip van Winkle.

6 Have a member of the class write a book report on *As A Driven Leaf*, a novel by Milton Steinberg.

7 Each member of the class should be assigned to report on some aspect of the Talmud, using *Everyman's Talmud*, by A. Cohen, as reference. Suggested topics are: The Justice and Mercy of God, The Soul, Free Will, Reward and Punishment, The Torah, Marriage and Divorce, Education, Master and Workman, Peace and Justice, Charity, Honesty, Forgiveness, Care of the Body, Criminal Law, and Civil Law.

8 Each member of the class should write an essay on "How the Talmud can help me apply the teachings of Judaism to my life."

9 Arrange a panel discussion on the question: "Should Jews be different?" Consider whether or not Jews should be involved in community controversies. For example, if a mass meeting is planned to protest an injustice, to what extent should Jews participate?

10 During the course of one week, select those news stories where Jews should be different, where they should not mix and join with others.

11 Invite a priest, a minister, and then your rabbi to speak to the class in succeeding weeks on "The Concept of Salvation," or "What must we do to be saved?"

SELECTED QUOTATIONS

A Golden Nail

The Talmud is the work which embodies the civil and canonical law of the Jewish people, forming a kind of supplement to the Pentateuch—a supplement such as took 1,000 years of a nation's life to produce. It is not merely a dull treatise, but it appeals to the imagination and the feelings, and to all that is noblest and purest. Between the rugged boulders of the law which bestrew the path of the Talmud, there grow the blue flowers of romance—parable, tale, gnome, sage; its elements are taken from heaven and earth, but chiefly and most lovingly from the human heart and from Scripture, for every verse and every word in this latter became, as it were, a golden nail upon which is hung its gorgeous tapestries.

EMANUEL DEUTSCH

Education for Democracy

It was the (Talmudic) study of the law in this spirit that ruled out all dictatorship and self-imposed authority in Israel. No matter how great the prestige of the rabbi who was always both administrator of justice and head of the academy, he could not silence the arguments of the poorest shoemaker or porter who knew the law. That was genuine democracy.

There is nothing the Jews dread more than the evil slogan of mobocracy: "One people, one state, one leader." There is nothing for which Jews yearn more than for the good tidings of democracy announcing: "One humanity, one divine Kingdom, One God."

MORDECAI M. KAPLAN

Helping Others

A traveler was crossing mountain heights of untrodden snow alone. He struggled bravely against the sense of sleep which weighed down his eyelids, but it was fast stealing over him, and he knew that if he fell asleep death would inevitably follow.

At this crisis, his foot struck against a heap lying across his path.

Stooping down, he found it to be a human body half-buried in the snow. The next moment he held him in his arms, and was rubbing and chafing the frozen man's limbs. The effort to restore another into life brought back to himself warmth and energy, and was the means of saving both.

The same law obtains in the realm of the soul. In order that our spiritual vitality may quicken into new life, we must help others in highest matters of faith and hope.

> Heaven's gate is shut
> To him who comes alone;
> Save thou a soul,
> And it shall save thine own.

JOSEPH H. HERTZ

This Too is for the Best

It is related of Nahum Gimso that he was blind in both eyes, that both his hands were crippled, that his feet were both cut off, and that the whole of his body was covered with leprosy. He lay stretched out in a crumbling house, and his legs were thrust into pots of water, that the ants might not get to him.

One day his pupils wanted to move his bed and the rest of his things into another house. Then he said: "My children, take the other things first and my bed last, for as long as I am in the house you may be certain that it will not fall." They did as he told them, and no sooner had they carried the bed out, than the house tumbled down.

Then his pupils said: "If you are so just a man, why do all these evil things overtake you?" "My children," he answered, "I brought them all on myself. One day, as I was going to the house of my father-in-law, leading three donkeys, one laden with provisions, one with wine, and one with rare fruits, I chanced to meet a poor man who stopped me and said: 'Master give me something to eat.' 'Wait,' I said, 'until I have unladen my donkey.' But I had not finished unlading the beast before the man died of starvation. Then I went and threw myself upon him, saying 'May my eyes, which had no pity on your eyes, lose their sight. May my hands, which had no pity on your hands, be crippled. May my feet, which had no pity on your feet, be cut off.' And my spirit was not at rest until I had said: 'May my whole body be covered with leprosy.'" His pupils replied: "Woe to us, that we see you in this condition." But he said: "Woe to me if you were not to see me thus."

The Talmud (Taanith)

For Whom the Sun Shines

Once Alexander the Great visited a king in an distant corner of the world. The king acted as a magistrate and invited his guest to sit beside him. Two men came before the court. One said: "I bought a house from this man, and while I was repairing it, I found a treasure. I offered to return it to him, but he refuses to accept it."

The other said: "I knew nothing of the treasure, and it does not belong to me. Since I sold him the house and lot, the treasure is his property."

The king said to one: "Have you a son?" and to the other: "Have you a daughter?" "Yes," was the answer from each. "Then," continued the king, "let them marry and keep the treasure as their dowry."

The king thereupon turned to Alexander and said: "Did I not judge wisely?" Alexander smiled and replied: "I would have cut off the heads of both fools and taken the treasure for myself."

The king shook his head. "Does the sun shine in your land?" "Yes," was Alexander's answer. "And does the rain fall in your land?" Again the answer was "Yes." "And are there cattle and sheep in your country?" "Yes," said Alexander.

"Then most assuredly," said the king, "it is only for the sake of the animals, and not for yours, that the sun shines and the rain falls."

The Midrash (Tanhuma)

Know Before Whom You Stand

In many of our temples and synagogues, there is an inscription above the Ark that reads: "Know before whom thou standest."

The source of this quotation is the Talmud. Rabbi Eliezer, the teacher of Akiba, was once asked by his disciples: "Teach us a way of life." He replied: "Have a constant prayer on your lips that no evil come to anyone through you. And when you pray, know before whom thou standest."

The Talmud (*Berochoth*)

Concerning Converts

Your question, why I do not try to make converts, has, I must say, somewhat surprised me. The duty to proselytize springs clearly from the idea that outside a certain belief there is no salvation. I, as a Jew, am not bound to accept that dogma, because, according to the teachings of the Rabbis, the righteous of all nations shall have part in the rewards of the future world. Your motive, therefore, is foreign to me; nay, as a Jew, I am not allowed publicly to attack any religion which is sound in its moral teachings.

MOSES MENDELSSOHN

SELECTED READINGS

Abrahams, Israel, *Chapters on Jewish Literature*, pp. 43–67.

Bildersee, Adele, *Jewish Post-Biblical History*, pp. 1–49.

Cohen, A., *Everyman's Talmud*, pp. 223–252.

Feuer and Glazer, *Jewish Literature Since the Bible, Book I*, pp. 40–62.

Newman, Louis, *Talmudic Anthology*.

Schechter, Solomon, *Studies in Judaism* (Third Series, The Talmud), pp. 194–225.

Universal Jewish Encyclopedia, The Talmud, Vol. X, pp. 160–168; The Midrash, Vol. VII, pp. 538–541.

Waxman, Meyer, *A History of Jewish Literature*, Vol. I, Chapters V–VI.

10

THE STILL, SMALL VOICE

Judaism in Action

Rabbi Mayer left his study and walked toward the classroom. This was to be the last session of the class before the summer vacation. He wondered how deeply he had impressed his students with the idea of Judaism as a way of life. Had he shown them that it is not enough to believe in Judaism, but that Judaism must be put into action at home, at play, at school, in their everyday relationships with others? Had they begun to understand the mystery of the Still, Small Voice?

His thoughts were interrupted by sounds of shouting, laughter, and running. The uproar was coming from his classroom. He opened the door, and in amazement he saw the students hopping around the room on one leg, bumping into each other, upsetting chairs, knocking books to the floor, as they shouted and laughed in wild commotion. Someone noticed the Rabbi and said, "Sh-Sh." Soon the room was quiet. The Rabbi waited patiently at his desk as the students picked up books and straightened out the chairs.

"What's this all about?" asked Rabbi Mayer. "Are you so happy that this is our last session that you are celebrating in advance?"

The class was relieved to see the Rabbi's good humor. Joseph grinned as he said: "We're sorry to kick up such a fuss, Rabbi, especially on the last day, but we remembered the story you told us about the pagan asking Hillel to explain Judaism while he stood on one foot. Someone said, 'I'd like to try it.' He lost his balance and started to hop. The rest of us decided to try it too, and that's when we all started hopping, laughing, and shouting. I hope you're not angry with us."

Rabbi Mayer smiled. "No, I'm not angry with you. I was planning to discuss the subject of Judaism in action today. But I didn't expect that much action!"

Judaism on One Foot

When the laughter subsided, the Rabbi said: "You remembered quite well that Hillel was asked to explain Judaism while the man stood on one foot. I hope you remember his answer too."

Almost all the members of the class indicated by a show of hands that they did remember. The Rabbi called on Sarah and she repeated the famous words of the golden rule:

> *Do not to your neighbor what you do not wish him to do to you.*

"Wasn't there something else?" asked Rabbi Mayer.
"I think I know," said Miriam.

> *This is the Law; all the rest is commentary.*

Rabbi Mayer opened his notebook. "The golden rule is also attributed to another great teacher, Akiba. The Talmud tells a story with an important lesson. Listen to it carefully."

It is related that a cart-driver came to Rabbi Akiba and said to him: "Rabbi, teach me the whole Torah all at once." He replied: "My son, Moses our teacher stayed on the Mount forty days and forty nights before he learned it, and you want me to teach you the whole of it all at once!

"Still, my son, this is the basic principle of the Torah: What is hateful to yourself, do not to your fellow man. If you wish no one to harm you in connection with what belongs to you, you must not harm him in that way. If you wish no one to deprive you of what is yours, you must not deprive your fellow man of what belongs to him!"

Rabbi Mayer looked up and said to the class: "If we left the story at this point, perhaps we would all nod in approval and agree with the teaching of Akiba. But the story is not yet ended. Will this be just a nice statement to the cart-driver, will it influence his actual behavior, and will he put this teaching into practice? Let us find out by reading the rest of the story."

The man rejoined his companions and they journeyed until they came to a field full of seed pods. His companions each took two, but he took none. They continued their journey and came to a field full of cabbages. They each took two, but he took none. They asked him why he had not taken any, and he replied: "Thus did Rabbi Akiba teach me: 'What is hateful to yourself, do not to your fellow-man.' "

"I get it," said Marvin. "It's easy to say you believe in the teaching of Hillel and Akiba. But the cart driver tried to put it into action. He didn't take the seed pods or cabbages because he wouldn't want anyone to take them out of his field."

"That's exactly it, Marvin." Rabbi Mayer walked around his desk to face the class. "This is the real meaning of the Still, Small Voice. The cart driver listened to it, and it told him that religion must be applied and used. It told him that Judaism has to be put into action! That's what we have been discussing all year—learning to hear the Still, Small Voice, listening to it tell us how to make Judaism our way of life.

Basic Judaism

"A long time ago, the rabbis in the Talmud tried to explain what Judaism means as a way of life. Rabbi Simlai taught this:

SIX HUNDRED AND THIRTEEN commandments were imparted to Moses—three hundred and sixty-five of which were prohibitions, answering to the number of days of the year, and two hundred and forty-eight positive commands, corresponding to the number of members in the human body.

Then came David and reduced them to ELEVEN, as it is written (Psalm 15):

> *Lord, who shall sojourn in Thy tabernacle?*
> *Who shall dwell on Thy holy mountain?*
> *He that walketh uprightly and worketh righteousness,*
> *And speaketh truth in his heart:*
> *That hath no slander upon his tongue,*
> *Nor doeth evil to his fellow,*
> *Nor taketh up a reproach against his neighbor;*
> *In whose eyes a vile person is despised,*
> *But he honoreth them that revere the Lord;*
> *He that sweareth to his own hurt and breaketh not his word;*
> *He that putteth not out his money on interest,*
> *Nor taketh a bribe against the innocent.*
> *He that doeth these things shall never be moved.*

Then came Isaiah and reduced them to SIX, even as it is written (Isaiah 33:15):

> *He that walketh righteously, and speaketh uprightly;*
> *He that despiseth the gain of oppression,*
> *That shaketh clear his hands from laying hold on bribes,*
> *That stoppeth his ears from hearing of blood*
> *And shutteth his eyes from looking upon evil.*

Then came Micah and reduced them to THREE, even as it is written (Micah 6:8):

> *It hath been told thee, O man, what is good,*
> *And what the Lord doth require of thee:*
> *Only to do justly, and to love mercy, and to walk humbly*
> *with thy God.*

Then came Isaiah once more and reduced them to TWO, as it is said (Isaiah 56:1):

> *Thus saith the Lord;*
> *Keep ye justice and do righteousness.*

Then came Amos and reduced them to ONE, as it is said (Amos 5:4):

> *Seek ye Me, and live.*

Rabbi Nahman, the son of Isaac, suggests another conclusion: Then came the prophet Habakkuk and reduced the commandments to ONE, which is the verse (Habakkuk 2:4):

> *The righteous shall live by his faith.*

"I remember that." Michael spoke up. "You told us about it when we started our study of Jewish ethics. That was when you were explaining about Judaism as a way of life, and you said it was one of the most important verses in the Bible."

"You have a good memory, Michael," Rabbi Mayer said. "I'm glad you remembered this verse. It is one of the most important verses in the Bible because it teaches that Judaism must be lived, and used, and not just talked about."

The Soapmaker and the Rabbi

A rabbi and a soapmaker once went for a walk together. The soapmaker said: "What good is Judaism? Look at the trouble and misery in the world, after thousands of years of teaching about goodness, truth and peace, after all the study and the sermons and the fine ideals! If Judaism is so wonderful and true, why should this be?"

The rabbi said nothing. They continued walking, until he noticed a child playing in the gutter. The child was filthy with soot and grime. Then the rabbi said: "Look at that child. You say that soap makes people clean, but see the dirt on that youngster. What good is soap? With all the soap in the world, that child is still filthy. I wonder just how effective or helpful soap is after all?"

The soapmaker protested and said, "But, Rabbi, soap can't do any good unless it's used!"

"Exactly," replied the rabbi. "So it is with Judaism. Judaism isn't effective unless it's applied and used!"

"That's what the prophet meant when he said that 'the righteous shall live by his faith,' " said Rabbi Mayer.

Visitor in Paradise

"Some people think that the purpose of religion is to prepare ourselves for the next world. Judaism says 'one world at a time.' It insists that we apply our faith to this world, that we build God's kingdom on earth, to bring about justice, brotherhood, and peace in this world.

"The Talmud teaches that the Commandments were given in order that man might live by them in this world. A beautiful legend tells of a man who yearned to behold Paradise while he was yet alive. Because of his piety and his persistence, his request was granted. In a dream he was escorted into Paradise. There he saw the sages seated around large tables meditating and studying the pages of the Bible and the Talmud.

"The man was amazed and he exclaimed: 'But I don't understand. Here the sages are studying and meditating on the teachings of God. Why, they are doing the very same thing that they did on earth!'

"It was then that a voice answered gently, saying: 'You do not understand, it is true. The sages are not in Paradise; Paradise is in the sages!'

"This story teaches that we can find our paradise in this world. Our heaven may be on earth. It can be in our hearts if we obey God's commandments and live up to His teachings.

The Secret of Religion

"We think that the secret of religion is hidden away somewhere, in some mysterious place. We think we must be great scholars or heroes performing spectacular deeds to hear the Still, Small Voice and to learn the commandments of God. The Book of Deuteronomy tells us that this is not true. It says:

> *This commandment which I command thee this day, it is not too hard for thee, neither is it far off. It is not in heaven, that thou shouldst say, "Who shall go up for us to heaven, and bring it to us, and make us to hear it, that we may do it?" Neither is it beyond the sea, that thou shouldst say: "Who shall go over the sea for us, and bring it unto us, and make us to hear it, that we may do it?" But the word is very*

nigh unto thee, in thy mouth, and in thy heart, that thou mayest do it.

"*That thou mayest do it:* these are the key words in Judaism, the words that help us solve the mystery of the Still, Small Voice. But what *is* the Still, Small Voice?

The Voice of Conscience

"Some people call it the Voice of Conscience. Dr. Erich Fromm a prominent psychiatrist, said:

One thing must be made clear. There are no prescriptions which can be found in a few books about the right living or the way to happiness. Learning to listen to one's conscience and to react to it does not lead to any smug and lulling "peace of mind" or "peace of soul." It leads to peace with one's conscience—not a passive state of bliss and satisfaction, but continuous sensitivity to our conscience and the readiness to respond to it.

"Dr. Fromm is right. Judaism has been teaching this for thousands of years. The Bible and the Talmud instruct us in the right way to live; they show us the way to happiness. One of the great purposes of Judaism is to help us learn to listen to the voice of conscience, a voice that shouts 'no' when we are tempted to do wrong, a voice that urges us to say 'yes' to the good way of life, to be unselfish, truthful, honorable and kind. Sometimes we refuse to listen to that voice, and we disobey God's commandments. Then we find ourselves faced with the consequences of our deeds. We discover that being deaf to the voice of conscience leads to unhappiness and disappointment. Those who listen to the voice and attempt to follow the teachings of the Torah will find that the Torah is:

a tree of life to them that hold fast to it.
Its ways are ways of pleasantness,
and all its paths are peace.

To Whom Does the Voice Speak?

"But Rabbi, what about people who aren't Jewish and don't have the Torah to follow? Doesn't the Still, Small Voice speak to them?" Joseph asked.

"When we began to study the 'Still, Small Voice,' you asked me that same question, Joseph, and I told you to wait until we had learned more about Judaism as a way of life. You had asked, 'Can't a person have a way of life that is decent, honorable and good without being Jewish? Do you have to be Jewish to know how to choose between right and wrong?'

"Actually, I believe that you can answer your own question now, Joseph. Am I right?"

"Yes, Rabbi, I think I can. I think I understand now what Judaism as a way of life means. It means everything we do and everything we say. It means using the teachings of the Bible, the Talmud and all the other sacred Jewish literature to make our lives better and happier. But what about my other question?"

"Joseph, I was hoping that you noticed something very significant about the teaching of Habakkuk. If you did," said the Rabbi, "it will give you a clue."

Joseph thought for a minute, and said: "*The righteous shall live by his faith.* That's the clue, isn't it? It doesn't say that only Jews should live by their faith, or that only Christians should live by their faith. It says 'the righteous,' meaning that all peoples of all religions shall live by their faith."

"You have stated it clearly and correctly, Joseph. That's exactly the way the rabbis interpret it. We believe that God's commandments were given through the people of Israel, through the Bible. But those commandments belong to all people. They are not the exclusive property of Jews. They help all God's children to choose between right and wrong. If a person is a Christian, he should live up to his faith. If he is a Moslem, he should live up to his faith. If he is a Jew, he should live up to his faith.

"The Still, Small Voice speaks to all peoples who try to apply the commandments of God. That's why the Talmud tells us that the Torah was given in seventy voices, corresponding to the seventy languages that were known at the time. Not only the Ten Commandments, but all the moral laws of God, apply to all peoples, whether or not they are of the Jewish faith.

"Perhaps that's why I become impatient with those who say that Judaism is a narrow religion, that Jews are concerned solely with the welfare and betterment of Jews. People who say that just don't understand Judaism.

Justice, Justice

"In the Bible we read: *Justice, justice shalt thou pursue.* The rabbis ask: 'Why is the word justice written twice?' Then they give the answer in a meaningful commentary.

To teach us that we must practice justice at all times, whether it it be for our profit or for our loss, and towards all men—toward Jews and non-Jews alike! Justice for the poor and justice for the rich. Justice for the scholar and justice for the unlearned. Justice for the stranger and justice for the home-born. Justice for those of your faith, and justice for those who are not of your faith. Jewish ethics makes no distinction between Jew and non-Jew in matters of justice. "The Holy One, blessed be He, rejects no human being. The portals are open, and anyone who desires may come and enter. . . ."

"Thus Judaism teaches us that the Voice of Conscience speaks to all peoples, if they will only listen. Justice, truth, mercy do not have tags and labels. We do not call them Jewish Justice, Jewish Truth, or Jewish Mercy. These ideas of justice, truth and mercy were given through Jewish literature, by God-inspired Jewish teachers, but they belong to all peoples and all faiths.

The Voice of Ethics

"Sometimes the Voice is called the Voice of Ethics. The dictionary defines ethics as 'the science of moral duty,' or more broadly, 'the science of the ideal human character, and the ideals and ends of human action.' This sounds very complicated. More simply, ethics deals with our behavior, the good that we do and the way we act. It is religion in action! It is living our faith! It is putting into deeds the ideals and teachings of religion.

"Many years ago a Christian teacher, George Foot Moore, wrote scholarly books on Judaism. His study of the Jewish faith prompted him to declare that 'there is no religion where man does not do something about it. Man must act out his belief.'

"Professor Samuel Cohon described the teachings of Judaism with these words: 'Religion is not so much knowledge of God, as godly living!' He then added: 'What distinguishes a religion from a system of science or philosophy is its concern with man's behavior.'

"What statement from the Bible teaches us very much the same thing?" asked Rabbi Mayer.

Bernard said: *"The righteous shall live by his faith."*

Michael said: "The words of Deuteronomy that you read to us: *That thou mayest do it.*"

Both boys spoke at almost the same time.

"Which is right, Rabbi?" they both asked, almost at the same time. Then they looked at each other and laughed.

Rabbi Mayer said: "It is difficult to choose between those two statements. You are both right. Both statements insist that Judaism is a religion of action. Both statements demand that Judaism be put to work in our lives.

"Yes, it is true that Judaism requires us 'to walk with God' just as Noah walked with God. Our sages make this very clear. They made Judaism a religion of action by proclaiming *Lo ha-midrash ikor, elah ha-maaseh;* It is not the theory or the teaching that counts most, but rather the doing, the action."

Rabbi Mayer continued. "During this year, I have noticed that some of you use the expression, 'live it up.' If I am correct, this means to have fun, to enjoy yourself, and to experience life to the fullest extent. Am I right?"

Heads nodded in agreement, and the Rabbi continued: "So many people believe that to be religious means to go around with a sad face, always to be serious, and never under any circumstances to permit yourself or others to enjoy anything. Judaism does not say this. According to the Jewish faith, we should all derive joy from life, and experience all possible happiness. The religious life is the happy life and, therefore, man is supposed to 'live it up.' But wait. . . .

"I see that some of you smiled when I said that we should 'live it up.' But that is exactly what Judaism demands of us. This doesn't mean that we should devote our lives to personal pleasures and physical enjoyment alone. When Judaism summons us 'to live it up,' it means that we must 'live it up'—to God. We must elevate our lives, our thoughts, and our deeds to the highest ideals, to the loftiest principles and teachings of God. It isn't enough to *talk* about our love for God. Do you remember the *midrash* where Israel was compared to an olive whose oil rises to the top? It is not enough for us to worship God with words. We prove our love for God by lifting our lives in the direction of God.

The Voice of God

"Whether we call the Voice the Voice of Conscience, or the Voice of Ethics, we believe that it is the Voice of God. The Voice of Conscience tells us to choose good and shun evil. The Voice of

Ethics tells us how to act. However we define it, we know that it is the Voice of God speaking to us within our hearts. This is the voice that urges us to choose good and reject evil. This is the voice that speaks against selfishness, cruelty, unclean thoughts and unclean deeds. This is the voice, the Still, Small Voice that speaks to us, that calls us to put Judaism to work, so that each of us may use it to enrich our lives and sanctify our years on earth with goodness and joy.

A Journey of Faith

"Sometimes we think of Judaism as a destination," said Rabbi Mayer. "We should think of it as a journey. This journey began at Sinai and has continued to the present time.

"We too have traveled far in our search for the mystery of the Still, Small Voice. I'm sure you all remember the unpleasant incident that made us aware of how important it is to apply the ethics of Judaism to our own lives. I'm so pleased and happy that the unfortunate incident has never been repeated. You have done your work honestly and capably, and I have enjoyed the opportunity to think with you about the magnificent teachings of our Jewish faith.

"Now, as the class comes to a close, perhaps we should take a little time to sum up. It might be interesting and challenging to check ourselves, and see if any of our opinions and attitudes about Judaism have changed.

SUMMING UP

1. The Voice of Jacob

"We began with the Voice of Jacob, and the question, 'What is a good Jew?' We decided that a good Jew could not be a splinter of the bat. He must not only know Judaism, but he must apply it at home, in the synagogue, at school, at play, in all his relationships with others. He must try to speak with the Voice of Jacob, and utter the noblest teachings of Judaism, shunning at all times the brutality and violence symbolized by the hands of Esau.

2. *The Voice of God*

"Tracing the belief in God from earliest times, we discovered that once God was regarded as a Master Magician. People were afraid of this jealous and vengeful God, and they tried to bribe Him with gifts and sacrifices. Then Judaism grew up, beyond the kindergarten belief in God, to a new and wonderful conviction— that we can show our love of God best by attempting to imitate His qualities of truth, justice, and holiness. We cannot see God, but we can behold His goodness. We hear the Voice of God when we obey His commandments and live His teachings in our every-day experiences.

3. *The Voice of Jewish Law*

"Very often we hear it said: 'I'm a Jew and proud of it!' It was through our study of the laws of the Bible that we learned how the poor, the stranger, the orphan, the sick, and the old were pro-tected in ancient times. The kindergarten belief in God gave way to the discovery that God represented justice and mercy, and de-manded justice and mercy from those who worshipped Him. Juda-ism was not a matter of ceremony and ritual alone. It meant the practice of honesty, truthfulness, and lovingkindness to all of God's children. Now we knew why we were proud of being identified with a kingdom of priests and a holy people. The Voice of Jewish Law had spoken to us, too.

4. *The Voice of Sinai*

"The tablets of the law, the Ten Commandments, took on new meaning for us. We had spoken about them, we had even memorized them, but after listening to the Voice of Sinai we understood what the Commandments have meant to mankind and what they should mean to us. These signposts of morality guide us to a life of goodness and decency. Our world would be completely changed if all the people who say they believe in the Commandments would actually practice them. The Decalogue is the greatest code of conduct ever given to mankind.

5. The Voice of the Prophets

"The Voice of the Prophets spoke to us with thunderous power. These were not foretellers, but forthtellers, speaking in the name of God, demanding justice and righteousness for all. They were men of rare courage, defying priests, nobles, and kings. They said that God did not want sacrifices. God did not want burnt-offerings. God wanted good deeds, kindness to the downtrodden, justice for the poor as well as the rich, and mercy for all.

"Some of you were surprised to learn that there are modern prophets, men and women of today who apply their faith to life, who refuse to be frightened by threats or violence as they speak out for truth, justice, and mercy. These prophets of yesterday and today are giants of the spirit. They summon us to: *do justly, love mercy and walk humbly with God.*

6. The Voice of the Psalmist

"The Voice of the Psalmist told us of the holiness of man. Man is not a robot; he is created in the image of God; he is 'but little lower than the angels.' In the Psalms we discovered hidden treasures of wisdom and truth. They revealed to us the quest for the divine, the eagerness and reverence of men who searched for the living God and found Him in the majesty of the heavens, in the wonder of the human body, and in the heart of man.

7. *The Voice of Wisdom*

"The Book of Proverbs offered us practical wisdom and helpful advice about Judaism as a way of life. It impressed us with the necessity of making our homes 'a little sanctuary' and heightening the sanctity of Jewish family life. We were told how man can conquer himself, how he finds light to see in the dark, how he obtains guidance to follow paths of righteousness and truth. The Voice of Wisdom gave us a plan and a moral code for a life of happiness and peace.

8. *The Voice of the Fathers*

"The *Pirke Aboth* revealed to us the teachings of the sages of Israel. We appreciated these sayings because they touched upon many familiar problems. The advice, 'Do not judge your neighbor until you are in his place,' was especially valuable. It helps us to be less severe in our judgments, and more lenient and merciful toward those who displease us. There were many other challenging teachings, such as 'Judge every man by the scale of merit'; 'Look not at the pitcher but at that which is in it.' The *Sayings of the Fathers* urged us to fulfill the ethical requirements of Judaism. We should not follow the crowd in wrongdoing, but strive for the strength of character that will enable us to apply the teachings of Judaism to every aspect of life.

9. *The Voice of the Rabbis*

"This voice spoke to us through the Talmud and the Midrash. Their stories and teachings showed us that Judaism is a universal religion, that God is the Father of all people. We saw how Israel has always stood fast before tyrants. We saw how its people made their most valuable contributions in times of pressure and persecution. The Talmud taught us that Jews must be different ethically and morally, that we must never join with others in deeds of cruelty and oppression. Just as the oil of the olive always rises to the top, so Israel must ever elevate itself in the direction of God, to those ideals that sanctify life with holiness.

10. *The Still, Small Voice*

"At last we learned that the Still, Small Voice is the sum of all the other voices we heard in the Bible and the Talmud. It tells us that Judaism is a living faith, that 'the righteous must live by his faith' every day and in everything he does. The religious life is the happy life. When we listen to the Voice of God, we are challenged and inspired to make our faith a living faith, to observe it and practice it at home, at play, and at work. All these voices join together to speak to us, to urge us to make the ethics of Judaism our way of life. All these voices, speaking to each of us through centuries of Jewish life and thought, give us the answer to the mystery of the Still, Small Voice.

CHECKING UP ON YOURSELF

Write an essay on "How the study of the ethics of Judaism has changed my opinions and attitudes about Judaism." Outline those things in the course that impressed you most. Mention any new ideas you developed in your search for the meaning of the Still, Small Voice.

CHECK YOUR REACTIONS

For Thine Own Sake

God, if I worship Thee in fear of hell,
Burn me in hell.
And if I worship Thee in hope of Paradise,

    Exclude me from Paradise;
    But if I worship Thee for Thine own sake,
    Withhold not Thine everlasting Beauty.
                           Rabiah

Does Judaism accept the meaning of this poem?

The Fires of Hell

A Baptist preacher once said in his sermon:

"There is a real fire in hell, as truly as you now have a real body—a fire exactly like that which we have on earth, except this, that it will not consume though it will torture you. You have seen the asbestos lying in the fire red-hot, but when you take it out, it is unconsumed. So your body will be prepared by God in such a way that it will burn forever without being consumed."

What does mature Jewish belief say about such a God, one who punishes His children with the fires of hell?

When God Says a Prayer

Even in the time of His anger, God remembers mercy, declares the Talmud. God is depicted as praying to Himself that His compassion be stronger than His wrath. "May it be My will that My mercy may subdue My wrath: and may My mercy prevail over My attribute of justice, so that I may deal with My children in the quality of mercy and enter on their behalf without strict justice."

How does this conception of God differ from that of a God of magic?

The Ten Commandments Are Too Controversial

A rabbi tells about the Temple trustee who urged him not to discuss any of the Ten Commandments in his sermon. When the rabbi asked for reasons, he was told that such a discussion might hurt the feelings of someone in the congregation. "What then shall I preach about?" asked the rabbi. "About Judaism," was the answer.

What would the Voice say to this Temple trustee?

Man, the Baboon, and the Grain of Sand

The late Justice Oliver Wendell Holmes once said:

"I think that the sacredness of human life is a purely municipal ideal of no validity. I see no reason for attributing to man a significance different in kind from that which belongs to a baboon or a grain of sand."

What does Judaism teach about the sacredness of human life?

Brotherhood Is a Lot of Hooey

During Brotherhood Week, a columnist wrote the following in the Santa Ana Register:

"As far as I am concerned, this brotherhood of man propaganda is a lot of hooey. It is about the same level as Democracy or Communism. You can hardly attend a meeting without hearing some sentimental old reprobate give vent to the Fatherhood of God and the Brotherhood of man.

What would be the attitude of Judaism to this statement? What do you think this columnist would say about justice for the Negro, about the rights of foreigners? What would you say?

What Asks Our Father

We live by Faith, but Faith is not the slave
Of text and legend. Reason's voice and God's,
Nature and Duty's, never are at odds.
What asks our Father of His children, save
Justice, mercy and humility;

> A reasonable service of good deeds,
> Pure living, tenderness to human needs,
> Reverence and trust, and prayer for light to see
> Our Lord God's guidance in our daily ways.
>   *John Greenleaf Whittier*

Which prophet expressed the same thought—Amos, Micah, Jeremiah, or Habakkuk?

Keep the Churches Out of Politics

"Lately some of the national church organizations have begun to meddle in politics. If the trend is not arrested, it can only lead to a loss of faith in churches and in clergymen. . . .

"For the decay in present-day morals and the deterioration of moral principle in governments throughout the world is perhaps largely due to the fact that many clergymen have been grossly negligent in their devotion to spiritual tasks. They have been diverted from their real duty. They have not fulfilled their true mission. They have become controversialists themselves—infected by the poison of pride and egotism."

DAVID LAWRENCE

What do you think the prophets of Israel, ancient and modern, would say about this statement?

Interesting Figures

Americans spend one and one-half billion dollars a year for the support of religious and social welfare organizations.

"That's a lot," you say. Perhaps, but look at these figures, too:
Twice as much (3.4 billion) goes for tobacco and cigarettes.
Four times as much (6 billion) is spent for horse racing.
Six times as much (8.8 billion) is spent on alcoholic beverages.

What new light do these figures throw on our contributions to charity?

Do you think that *tzedakah* (justice) is a better term than charity? What does Judaism think about this?

I Your Friend

When Sergeant Albert L. Howard returned from Korea after being held as a prisoner of war, he told about a strange and heart-warming experience. He had been hit in the right arm by a piece of shrapnel. Suddenly, he noticed an enemy soldier coming toward him. Quickly he switched his gun to his other hand, but the enemy knocked the gun to the ground. Looking into the muzzle of a burp gun, he waited, expecting the bullet that would end his life.

What happened next was the strange part of the story. The enemy soldier helped his American prisoner-of-war off the ground, put a blanket around him, and in broken English said: "I your friend." As a soldier, every American was his enemy. As a human being, he could look upon another human being with mercy and say: I your friend.

What does Judaism teach us about the treatment of enemies? Do you think this soldier has a share in God's love?

Music of Religion

We defend religion too much. Vital religion, like good music, needs no defense, but rendition. A wrangling controversy in support of religion is precisely as if the members of the orchestra should beat folks over the head with their violins to prove that the music was beautiful. But such procedure is in no way to prove that music is beautiful.

A Christian minister, Harry Emerson Fosdick, made that statement. Would Judaism agree or disagree?

The Touch of Every Living Thing

Could I be happy in a suffering world?
By day, by night, in dreams I feel the touch
Of every living thing; to me, man, beast
The stones and grasses of the field, all cry
With mute, imploring eyes they cry
To me, and yet the answer must be His.

Richard Beer Hoffman

What, in your opinion, is the answer of God?

Albert Einstein's Credo

The striving after knowledge for its own sake, the love of justice verging on fanaticism, and the quest for personal independence— these are the motivating traditions of the Jewish people which cause me to regard my adherence thereto as a gift of destiny . . . as long as we remain devoted servants of truth, justice and freedom, we shall not only continue to exist as the oldest of all living peoples, but we shall also, as hitherto, create through productive effort, values which shall contribute to the ennobling of mankind.

In what way is Albert Einstein's credo a good summary of the ethics of Judaism?

Be Strong and We Will Strengthen Each Other

The members of the class finished their work, and waited for the Rabbi to dismiss them. It was almost time for the bell.

Rabbi Mayer glanced at the clock. "We have just a few more minutes," he said, "and now it is time to say *Hazak V'nischazake*. How many of you know what this means? Jonathan, I see your hand is up. Will you tell us?"

"It means 'Be strong and we will strengthen each other,' said

Jonathan. "And these words are read after the reading of each of the Five Books of Moses is concluded. Isn't that right?"

"Yes it is, Jonny," said Rabbi Mayer. "The section ends with the hope that the inspiration found in that portion of the Bible will strengthen us to obey God's teachings and commandments. Each of us has the power to help the other. If each of us will be strong, if each of us will cleave to these teachings, we will add strength to strength. We will support and uphold each other in making Judaism our ethical way of life.

"And now, until the next school year, it is time for us to say goodbye. I hope each of you will have a happy summer, and I hope that many of you will attend Sabbath Services during the summer months. Until we meet again: *Hazak, Hazak V'nischazake.* Be strong! Be strong, and we will strengthen each other!"

The bell rang. The members of the class walked up to the desk to thank Rabbi Mayer for their unusual and interesting year of study.

As the students approached the door, they noticed that the Rabbi had turned the portable blackboard around, and on it was written in large letters:

And behold, the Lord passed by, and a great and strong wind rent the mountains, and broke in pieces the rocks before the Lord; but the Lord was not in the wind; and after the wind an earthquake; but the Lord was not in the earthquake; and after the earthquake a fire; but the Lord was not in the fire; and after the fire—A Still, Small Voice!